Volume 1

Remember and Transform

The Story of Finding Empowerment Through Education

A Plan of Action for a New Vision of Economics & Education in the Black community

AF808660

For information regarding special discounts for bulk purchases, buying New Element courses for your home, school, or program, or to schedule workshops, education consultations, or speaking engagements, contact:

Finding Empowerment Through Education, LLC
100 South Juniper 3rd Floor - #6107 Philadelphia, PA 19107 |
Toll-free: 1-833-313-FETE (3383) | Lori@FETEPhilly.com

Copyright © 2022 by **Lori Michelle Chambers** All rights reserved Published by beyondthebookmedia.com All rights reserved. No part of this publication may be reproduced, distributed, or transmitted in any form or by any means, including photocopying, recording, or other electronic or mechanical methods, without the prior written permission of the publisher, except in the case of brief quotations embodied in critical reviews and certain other noncommercial uses permitted by copyright law. For permission requests, write to the publisher, addressed "Attention: Permissions Coordinator," at the address below. Limit of Liability/Disclaimer of Warranty: While the publisher and author have used their best efforts in preparing this book, they make no representations of warranties with respect to the accuracy or completeness of the contents of this book and specifically disclaim any implied warranties or merchantability or fitness for a particular purpose. No warranty may be created or extended by sales representatives or written sales materials. The advice and strategies contained herein may not be suitable for your situation. You should consult with a professional where appropriate. Neither the publisher nor author shall be liable for damages arising here from. Beyond The Book Media, LLC Alpharetta. GA www.beyondthebookmedia.com The publisher is not responsible for websites that are not owned by the publisher.
ISBN 978-1-953788-36-8 (Printed)

Volume 1

Remember and Transform

Lori Michelle Chambers

Dedication

This book is dedicated to:

My dad, mom, sister, brother, grandparents, and the rest of my family - the divine gift of life-long friends and unconditional love.

Table of contents

Synopsis

The state of the current education system is disastrous. The coronavirus pandemic caused an upheaval in an already flawed institution. This system has failed you, me, and our children. Our neighborhood schools were converted into juvenile detention centers before our very eyes before the national shutdown.

Removing the trades, music, and the arts caused a downward spiral. Our strong teachers were our lifejackets and our first line of defense in the school-to-prison pipeline. The best teachers endure years of psychological abuse, personal suppression, dwindling resources, and minimal parental support. Adding insult to injury, most are underpaid and under-appreciated.

Eventually, moving on to other positions in more affluent neighborhoods/districts and thus creating a gaping hole that creates a myriad of missed opportunities for children of color. There is a unique essence and way of reaching children that our best Black teachers possess.

As a result, a prudent parent must strive to live in a favorable area in order to enroll their child into an adequate school; that supports their best chance at success. Unfortunately for our children, most schools in our neighborhoods have poor academic performance, and the climate is generally unsafe.

Is this just the way of things in America, academic capitalism, or is this a prescribed, cyclical death sentence delivered to the Black community through socially engineered oppression? Parents have limited options in accessing a full-scale, adequate, relevant, and easily applied curriculum to convert to home environments.

Children who are neglected are on life support. Who is accounting for these lost children and assisting the parents? While some of us are the busiest we have been in our lives, in contrast, other lives have come to a halt.

The heavy artillery social assault rifles of racism and classism delivered by kin or foe have blasted holes in the façade of the American dream as well as the bodies of Black brothers and sisters in front of our very eyes. Where does it end? What is the solution for the devastating cycles of poverty, mental illness, violence, and hopelessness we experience in this nation? This is a real-time collaborative plan of action, not just for the people but also for those who want to create change.

Introduction

I am Lori Chambers, the founder of ***Finding Empowerment Through Education***. We operated as a nonprofit organization from 2007 to 2016. I also was a licensed Life, Health, and Accident Insurance producer and many other professions during those years.

As a nonprofit, our conceptual framework was to exist as an umbrella organization to multiple education programs, operating simultaneously, each targeting specific skills normally left underdeveloped in today's homes and school systems.

Over those years, my concepts for the program I was directing, Life Sciences, expanded dramatically. I began to recognize the gaping holes in the overall system of education-work-retirement in America and soon realized that it takes a wraparound approach between business development, investing/financial planning, in concert with the people taking control of teaching and cultivating the minds of young people, that could truly eliminate the social constraints of today.

With that realization grew ***New Element***, the next generation of the Life Sciences program. ***New Element*** is an ever-evolving curriculum designed to be taught to all ages. Fun should not end just because we are no longer children, just as education should not end when we are adults.

In fact, we are reversing the paradigm and allowing our children to teach us some things beyond our normal comprehension. We are revolutionizing how it feels to learn; what it looks like to be "in class." We are the future of education!

Preface

I am one of the most dangerous people on the planet. From the perspective of the powers that be who wish to maintain worldly power and oppress the people through corrupt systems, my ideas are deadly, ones that could empower a nation. I am not playing. And I am not the only one. There are many like me. Mostly unsung, mostly underpaid, mostly dearly departed, but around, nonetheless. It is integral that we be courageous in this day in time, for there is a war of the mind at hand.

I write this book primarily to reach and reassure people out there who hold an ideal in their hearts. One that, by this world's standards, is not realistic or seems too big of an undertaking. For some of you, the case may be that like-minded individuals are not in your friends and family circle. You may be an outlier. You may be the black sheep. You may be alienated in your own home.

But I have learned one thing from experience; you are usually the one to break the generational curse. The ones whose empathy cannot allow them to shrug off the staple ills of the world as a normal occurrence and a helpless plight. We are not born to struggle. We were not born to live humbly, silently, miserably, or invisibly.

It is our God-given birthright to co-create our experience with our maker. We were designed to resist the programming induced upon us before we could consent. It is not a curse to be different; it is a gift we have been granted by God.

> **"I'm not saying I'm gonna change the world, but I guarantee that I will spark the brain that will change the world."**
>
> **– Tupac Shakur**

Prologue

The atrocity that stings the most is the one you are here to impact. What stung the most for me was going to school every day from age four to seventeen. The ongoing agony, anxiety, and inadequacy I internalized left me depressed and disillusioned at pivotal points in my life.

I hated school, even from day one. Kindergarten was my first structured socialization (I was fortunately spared the perils of daycare and kept snug at home). My first memory at school is a toy being viciously snatched out of my hand by a madwoman. She was five and clearly had experience in getting what she wanted.

It was only a half-day of kindergarten, but 8:45 to 11:45 felt like a whole 9 to 5 for me. I would be so ready to get back to my lunch and *David the Gnome* on Nickelodeon I'd be sick to my stomach. I was not fitting in. I was not talking. I was salty.

Even "Who Stole the Cookie from the Cookie Jar?" around the circle gave me panic attacks. The circle did NOT feel like a safe space. It was just overwhelming. We would all be sitting around patting, clapping, and snapping to the beat of "Who Stole the Cookie from the Cookie Jar?" and when they got to Lori?! I messed up the whole rhythm!

The room would fall silent, and I would just sit there with everyone staring at me as if I had no clue how to play the game or what to say. I did, but I did not like participating. So, my teacher, Ms. Solo, would help me along. She would say, "C'mon, Lori say, 'Who me?'" Then I would repeat "Couldn't be" with my eyes to the floor and barely opening my mouth. It was torture from my point of view, but I kept chugging along.

I recall being tested for the MG (mentally gifted) program 2-3 times between 1st and 3rd grade and failing to be accepted all three times (see, I don't count well). And that really pissed me off. It was not until I read Sister Souljah's autobiography *No Disrespect* ten years later that I began to fully understand my resentment.

The child's mind knows what it cannot yet articulate. It was blatant bullshit. Children being picked out and given enriching experiences while the rest are herded and left in wonderment when they return looking all happy and refreshed and shit.

In short, it creates a class system amongst children. The haves and the have-nots. And how are the haves supposed to feel? "Well, I guess this is a meritocracy. I guess them niggas better pull theyself up by they bootstraps (which is physically impossible, by the way; please do not attempt to do that)." This is the attitude our schooling intended to be imprinted upon us and carried for the rest of our lives, and by and large, it is.

A Philadelphia public-school classroom is a perfectly suppressive environment. In 1991, at the height of the crack epidemic, placing thirty children in one room for the better part of eight hours seemed overwhelming for one teacher to manage and normally left quite a few of us to fend for ourselves.

Me being especially shy carried the unfortunate duty of having to speak up to get what I needed. I was not taught that at home. I usually prayed for an invisibility cloak to be dropped from heaven to get me through each day.

One day I let my anxiety get the best of me, it was bathroom break time, and my teacher seemed to be in a bit of a bad mood. She stood at the front of the class, surveying our seats with raised hands. I put my hand up halfway, and everyone's hands raised, and she started calling students up by twos and writing hall passes for them.

After about four rounds of this, the teacher said, "Anyone else?" I really had to go bad enough to go in the first few rounds, but everyone was so eager that the teacher didn't even look at me. Because she seemed ready to end bathroom time, I lowered my hand and waited for her next lesson to resume.

I don't remember how much time went by, but I started to get warm. Then out of nowhere, one of my classmates jumped up, screamed, and pointed in my direction, "Lori peein' on herself!" It was only then, amid the screaming, hysterical laughter, and desks moving, that I could hear the drops hitting the floor from my seat.

Even today, if I speak to certain classmates from Emlen Elementary School, they still like to remind me, "Lori, remember that time you peed on yourself!?" I do.

That embarrassed six-year-old girl is still inside of me, still unsure how to ask for what she needs and hoping people won't point and laugh at her for things she can't control. I remember a lot, forgot a lot more. But what is forgotten isn't lost; it's within me. I can transform my experience, which is the world as I know it. And so can you.

Part one is my journey through my schooling in the Philadelphia School District written in creative nonfiction story form for you, the reader, to build a relationship with me. I want you to understand my perspective on life and, more importantly, to assess my being through my narration.

Part two is a transition into applying my concepts in my young adult years. Part three is written in essay form and highlights my evolution to my current perspective, formed from observations and evaluations of my own experiences and study.

Part 1

The Recollection

Chapter 1

Who is Lori?

"Who's the black sheep, what's the black sheep? Know not who I am, or when I'm coming, so you sleep"
-(Sheep)

1st Grade

I didn't like the first grade. I felt like my teacher, Mrs. Graham, had favoritism toward the short children. I was quite tall for my age, with awfully long, skinny legs and knobby knees. She never picked me up and swung me in delight like she did the two to three munchkins in our class.

This act didn't just spark jealousy but was a reminder that I, the quiet, awkward, dark skin girl, was last in line for attention and fun. I was a girl by gender definition, but I felt more like a blur of a self, maybe an inanimate object to be ignored or picked up when necessary.

The interesting thing about life at that time was that it was lived in segments, like separate worlds where a different version of me would emerge. I did not feel this alienation from the kids I grew up with on my block. I wasn't very high up on the totem pole.

I had been kicked off my share of porches and made to be "on ends" countless hours of playing jump rope without barely a chance to get to jump. But at home, I had no problem directing any feelings of slight into my fists.

We would fight like cats and dogs on my block, Mayland Street. I grew up on a one-way block of row homes in Germantown. We would play wrestling out in the street and in our front yards. The yard was the perfect setting for wrestling because we had a railing around our porches that allowed for climbing the ropes and delivering a *Flying Elbow Drop* to an opponent.

5 out of 10 times our fake matches erupted into real brawls, much like in professional wrestling in the days of old. One time, a match between me and one of the other younger girl wrestlers, Regina, resulted in her entire family walking up the block and knocking on my door to "clear the air."

I probably blacked out in the ring. All I know is by the end of our match she was disheveled and red. Everyone got silent as she cried up the street to tell her family. This was not good. Gina had a lot of cousins our age and older.

I ran into the house, into me and my mom's room, out of breath and slightly panicked, and immediately went to the corner and started playing with my *Mr. Potato Head.* After a few minutes, I heard a husky, police-like knock on the front door and a collection of footsteps and grumbles. My heart sank into my stomach. "Me and my mommy was going to have to whoop all they asses," I thought to myself.

At home, I was much like the shy, invisible child I was in school. Most of my time at home was spent in the shadows. Some of my best times were spent in the comfort of my private lair under the dining room table. I didn't start talking until I was three. My brother was ten years older than me, and my sister was fourteen years older.

I tried to live life vicariously through them, but I wasn't allowed to be around for much of what they were doing. But the music was good. Once in a while, one of them would let me chill in their room and I'd pick up the entire vibe. The Public Enemy and De La Soul reverberating from their speakers was infectious.

My brother had me memorize and perform "Cold Lampin'" on demand. My sister went away to college in 1989 when I was four years old, and it broke my heart. She provided me with exposure to the world. With her gone, that meant I would not go on as many outings. I loved to go anywhere on the subway. The underground dungeon scene reminded me of the *Teenage Mutant Ninja Turtles.*

My transition to school and my sister to college could have been worse had it not been for television. My mother and I would post up and watch all the goodies. I was watching *The Simpsons* shorts on *The Tracey Ullman Show* weekly, thinking to myself, "This should be an entire show."

We used to watch *Murphy Brown, Perfect Strangers, Mork & Mindy, The Mary Tyler Moore Show, Arsenio Hall, David Letterman, The Golden Girls, In the Heat of the Night, Twin Peaks, ER,* you name it, I was watching it, trying to figure out how life worked in every aspect.

Me and mom-mom had our own special TV relationship. Me and the rest of the young kids got called in when the streetlights came on, and we always protested for a little more time, especially if we were really immersed in a game. But when it was Friday, all our parents had to say was it was 8 o'clock, and we were all dashing home realizing that we were hungry and to watch *TGIF*[1].

My tradition with mom-mom was to watch *Family Matters* together. But that wasn't it. We could laugh all episode long together watching *Martin*. When I got older, and a door connected my and mom-mom's room, we would watch *The Outer Limits* together from our own rooms. Then we'd both have crazy dreams that night and talk about them in the morning.

Once my sister went off to college, there was enough room in our house for me to have my own room next to mom-mom's.

But I resisted that transition. I now realize that my insecurity about sleeping alone and my mortal fear of the dark were probably exacerbated by my difficult transition to school.

I think I finally moved out of my mom's crib and into my own place around 1993 when I was about eight. I still sucked my thumb, but I was to refrain most of the day until downtime or bedtime. One night I lay in bed intending to end my habit. I closed my eyes and decided to lay on my hand. When I woke up in the morning, my arm was asleep, at my side with no trace or slobber. I'd overcome my very first addiction.

With just me in the house now, it was even quieter than before. My mother told me that my brother was away at Glen Mills for being a juvenile delinquent and that Angie was doing well at the University of Delaware. So, it was down to us three ladies: me, my mom, and mom-mom.

I wasn't quite sure what my brother had done. But he was in trouble often. I recall being with my mom as she walked up to Germantown High, burned up mad once after she had been called by the school about his behavior. I also remember my brother coming home bloody and bruised because cops beat him up. There was a billy club kept on the China cabinet for some reason. I was never sure if it signified our getting the best of the system one day or a reminder to fear it?

I remember cops being in our house because they were called on my brother by my mom and mom-mom. I could never forget to this day how upset my brother was at them. It was an all-out nervous breakdown. His stress and heartbreak damn near suffocated me, his tear-filled face and cracking voice screeching, "Why would you call them on me?" I did not understand the systematic brutality and genetic annihilation of Black men at this age, but I understood this circumstance to be an act of betrayal.

I was always listening. I remember the male-bashing on daytime television from *Sally Jessie Rafael, Geraldo,* and *Phil Donahue* and the claps and comments in the living room after certain topics. I knew that a man not with his children had to pay something called child support to the mother. I was wondering where mine was.

When I would get a hold of a Christmas catalog and lounge on the couch with a marker circling my wish list as commercials interrupted my weekday afternoon programming, I always had doubts. I knew that my family did not celebrate Christmas, but I couldn't help but get into the spirit, with my birthday being only two days afterward.

I would imagine the tree, lights, and smell of warm cookies on the eve and go to sleep happy that night, hoping for a miracle. One year I believe I did awaken to a traditional pile of wrapped gifts, but then again, I could have fabricated that memory. Either way, it's true in my heart.

I do not have early memories of my father. I find this fact very strange because my long-term memory is extensive. But I know from stories he's told me that he was there during my infancy. My earliest memories are from the perspective of my highchair in the kitchen watching mom-mom come in from work in a white cooking outfit. I would stare at her, and she would look at me and ask me, "What you lookin' at?"

I didn't really feel my father's absence except when it was the reason I couldn't have certain things. When it was time to go school shopping, I couldn't get anything I picked out for myself. It was a push and pull and temper tantrum the entire way.

When toy commercials would come on and break the daytime tv cast, my requests were denied citing my not having a dad to help pay for those expensive things. So, I began to inquire, "Where is my child support?"

Once, my mom told me that there was no point in trying to get child support from my dad because he would just tell the judge that he had no money. I was NOT satisfied with this explanation. Besides these rare flare-ups, my dad's exact whereabouts never came out. It didn't seem abnormal because I don't remember a time otherwise. It remained that way until we were reintroduced a few years later.

2nd & 3rd Grade

Mrs. Donsky in the second grade was great. She somehow made me feel like an individual while in her class. I remember feeling okay in her classroom. Mrs. Donsky is the undisputed champion Simon in Simon Says. She was one of those Simons whose more like a verbal puppet master. She would have us on a string knocking us out of the game one by one with her smooth, staccato, unorthodox delivery! Oh, it still gets me excited just thinking of it!

Third grade might as well have been high school for me. I was already feeling lost in math since the first grade when I could never figure out which way the shark's mouth had to face for the number to be greater than or less than. So, when I got to Mrs. Johnson's class, I knew it would be an uphill battle. It was survival. My strategy was staying under the radar, and the name of the game was underachievement.

Third grade felt like boot camp. Mrs. Johnson demanded that we line up and file through the halls quietly every time, no exception. She was one of those no-nonsense teachers with an edge. From her giraffe-themed, wide-leg, flowy pants walking up from behind us, smacking us upside the head with a rolled-up newspaper, to her failing the entire class three times for failing the same test on abbreviations, Ms. Johnson demanded excellence.

This was my final year of being tested for the MG program, and I was always talking to myself in my head, asking myself if I was smarter or cooler than my classmates I compared myself with. I was always in the back of the girl's line because I was tall. Size order showed control through uniformity.

During this time, our teacher would still lead us to our class transfers, and how we behaved in the hallway "in public" was a big deal in the social status and hierarchy of the teachers I observed. The more control you had over your classroom, the more you were respected.

One day we were lining up inside the classroom in size order to go to lunch. A girl named Christian was the same height as me, so we interchanged who stood in front of who casually. On this day, she insisted on standing in front of me so that I would be the last person in line.

Usually, it was a seamless exchange between us, so I was wondering why she preferred to be in front. The girl's line was longer than the boy's line and reached back towards Mrs. Johnson's desk and a folding table just behind it.

With Mrs. Johnson in the front of the line settling everyone down for departure, Christian stepped out of line and went straight behind the teacher's desk, grabbed a bag of chips from the pile sitting on the table, and stuffed it in her windbreaker jacket.

By the time we returned from recess, it was evident Mrs. Johnson knew something was amiss. She had either counted the bags, seen that the chips had been disturbed, or maybe a bag had even fallen. I was not sure because it all had happened so fast. I didn't get a photograph in my mind of the crime scene. But what had not dawned on me was that I was about to get caught up in the investigation.

I was accused by Christian, who provided a phony eyewitness testimony of me snagging the chips. And to put the cherry on top, claimed that it "had to be me since I was the last person in line." I was being framed!! I did not and could not defend myself. I think the level of appalled I was to even be considered for such a thing muted me. I took the heat for it. And later that year, she ended up getting into MG, and I did not.

This experience taught me that the system is rigged against people like me. It really does not matter what you do or don't do for the eyes of the world. Truth just won't prevail because it is logical. You have to fight for it to be acknowledged.

You must advocate for your own stance. I did not do that, and I always wondered if that was a trait that kept me out of the gifted program. I have thought about this incident a lot over the years. Now turning 35 in a week as I write these words, I see it a little differently.

I feel like my teacher did know that I wasn't the one who stole the chips. Maybe she let me go down for it to show me what happens when I don't defend myself. I'd like to believe it was the latter because Mrs. Johnson believed in planting seeds in our minds.

Mrs. Johnson gave me my first D. I almost had a nervous breakdown. I didn't realize that my self-worth clung to my report cards; they were the only thing that gave me the confidence to carry on each day in school.

The 'D' was in handwriting; my penmanship was not the best. I also knew in the back of my mind that by the time I would be writing anything of importance, it would not be in cursive. In fact, it would probably be typed out. Yes, I realized that in the 3rd grade.

But my soul was crushed nonetheless by the scathing review of my work. The rest of my grades were B's and C's, not the A's and B's I was accustomed to. My mom wasn't a big fan of parent-teacher conferences, but I'm pretty sure that Mrs. Johnson damn near subpoenaed her up to Emlen Elementary School.

At the conference, I recall Mrs. Johnson telling my mom that I still have not broken out of "my shell." All of my previous teachers used that turn of phrase to describe me verbally or in writing. I only remember her saying something about running away from achievement before I stopped comprehending the conversation consciously and zoned out, only to realize I was crying hysterically.

They wrapped up their conversation and decided it was a good idea to talk to my previous teacher from the second grade, where I thrived, Mrs. Donsky, about the situation. Mrs. Johnson called over to room 213 from her classroom wall phone, then sent us on our way.

We walked around to the wing, where most of the second-grade classrooms were located, and entered Mrs. Donsky's room, still teary and distraught. I went right over to her, and she consoled me. She asked me what was wrong; I didn't have a response. I couldn't understand or articulate just what was going on with me. But just having her stoop down to my height level, look at me, hold my arms and ask felt very comforting, like the solution.

For that one moment, I didn't feel like I was drowning. The details of her meeting with my mother are blurry after that. I just remember she tried to give me the best encouragement she could, and I appreciated it.

I did a lot of studying in Mrs. Johnson's class before and after that grading period. Her tests were very rigorous, and I stayed up late with my mom practicing for spelling tests or working on projects a lot. It gave me confidence going into the weekly test prepared.

But one Friday after lunch, when we usually would take our spelling test, Mrs. Johnson flipped the script on us. We walked into the classroom where most of the desks had been set aside and the others were configured to form lanes that ran from the back of the classroom up to the chalkboard.

Everyone was all giddy and excited about what was to come. I was beginning to feel nauseous. Mrs. Johnson was one of the last of a dying breed of teachers in the hood. It was straight Joe Clark style. I can imagine her being propositioned to leave her third-grade class to rehabilitate Eastside High.

The stage was set. Instead of taking the test the normal way, our teacher explained, we would be having a challenge. She counted us off into teams and explained we had to race to the board and spell the word she called out correctly to earn points for our team.

"Easy enough," I thought, but I did not like the group setting and competition of it all. I already saw the cliques forming within the teams. I was not having fun at this point, just looking at everyone else's excitement. This was going to be a long afternoon.

Because I was fast and loved running, the game didn't start too bad; I scored the first points easily. Midway through the game, the tide was turning, and the lead my team had built began to dwindle. Some of the more difficult words from the list were coming out, showing who was prepared and who wasn't.

As fate would have it (or Mrs. Johnson), the final word landed on my turn. And the word was Colonel. Mommy had gone over this word with me several times, and I knew good and well exactly how to spell it and that it was not spelled the way it's pronounced. I actually was very proud of myself for having mastered that word. I looked over at the person I'd be squaring off with. I can't recall which of my classmates it was or if that glance I took affected my performance. But let's just say I was fine at first, then I choked.

I ran up the lane with the quickness, my team cheering me on, tasting sweet victory on their tongues. I get up there and start writing real slow for some reason. Then I started looking over at what the other person was doing. I couldn't believe it. He wasn't sure how to spell it! He was putting an "r" in it, so all I had to do was write the word. Game Over.

But I couldn't bring myself to do it. With everyone looking at me, I thought about it once again and looked over at what the other person was doing. Finally, I copied the same letters my competitor wrote down, then put the chalk down. That is my final answer.

Everyone was let down. I didn't look anyone in the eye for the rest of the day. I sat praying for my invisibility cloak to drop down from heaven on me. I wondered what kept me from writing down the correct answer.

Was it the many eyes on me and the anticipation of the shouts and cheers all directed towards me that gave me anxiety? Or was it that I felt that even if I would have won the game for my team that I would still go back to being just Lori once this moment had passed.

Or this newly formed winning streak would motivate me towards excelling more. Then I'd get teased for being too smart or disliked for being a know-it-all. Either way, I was uncomfortable with the attention that came with achievement, and I avoided it at all costs.

Mrs. Johnson was just as passionate about history, music, and culture as she was about language arts. One of the most important moments in my life is one lesson she taught us in class towards the end of the day. She resumed instruction after breaks by smacking us upside the head with the newspaper she had just been reading at her desk.

But once she got our attention, she unrolled 10x13 sized posters of several statues and sculptures from Ancient Egypt. There were photographs of people with big lips and wide noses and some with dreadlocks and afros. "Look at you!" she said. "This is you you are looking at. Touch your nose. This is your bloodline," she said passionately, looking each of us in the eye as she walked the room. I don't think I ever looked at life the same after that.

In the springtime, Mrs. Johnson invited one of her friends to come to teach us songs on her guitar. This was thrilling, and I didn't feel any social pressure. I thought I looked like the singing teacher. She had brown skin, kind small eyes, and long locks. She came to teach us "Redemption Song" by Bob Marley.

Every line we memorized resonated so much within my soul. Mrs. Johnson taught us "Better Days" by Dianne Reeves on her own, off her cassette player she'd place on a desk in the center of the room. We'd gather around and learn the melody and words each day for about 45 minutes until we were ready to perform it at our Grandparent's Day assembly.

Although we had learned the entire song, Mrs. Johnson made it abundantly clear that we were not supposed to sing the song's ending at the assembly because it might bring down the mood. But when our third-grade class got up there and heard our voices resound throughout the auditorium, we really started to feel the words, and it moved us.

We totally disregarded our teacher's instructions and deviated from her orchestrating hands, and the music fading out in our little, solemn voices sang, "Later that year, at the turn of spring, heaven-sent angels down and gave grandma her wings..." (Reeves). Mrs. Johnson was so embarrassed and quickly climbed the side stairs up the stage to whisk us off back behind the curtains. I don't know why, but we had to get that out for some reason.

In hindsight, I don't think any of the grandparents in the audience were offended. Everybody knows how the song goes, plus we were all probably rehearsing at home for weeks. And a lot of us were raised by our grandma or co-parented, like in my case.

Grandparents as heads of the household and primary caregivers remain a norm to this day within America's lower-class families. The drug epidemic inundated a lot of parents and ravaged the family structure. The grandparent's assembly was the only event I recall my grandmother attending in an elementary school outside of graduation.

It was a good feeling seeing her happy when we all got home and settled. I can imagine my classmates were proud as well. Most of us revered our grandparents as our home's foundation and because of all the love they poured into us. Through music, Mrs. Johnson created everlasting memories for all her students.

My mother was really into politics that year. She was all in for Chaka Fattah. And I remember my mom being pretty into Bill Clinton as well. I can picture her dark brown hair curled up against her head, walking up to the polls at Mallory Playground to vote that year.

All the commercials and his saxophone playing on *Arsenio Hall* pandering to Black people made me look at the TV skeptically. My mom was excited at this time, but I was always a cynic. I still was in the habit of drawing out torture instruments on the blank pages of my activity pad while watching the 5 o'clock news with them.

Mrs. Johnson was all in for Chaka Fattah. She used to have this dance move and African-sounding cadence that came on after each time she said his name. She'd start a slow shimmy to the ground saying "Chaka Fattah," in a low militaristic tone, and then about a four-count later, she'd rise back up to a fully standing position while clenching her fist and growling, "Yesss," letting the S linger in power for a few seconds.

It seemed a little brainwashed to me, but I've learned there is a thin line between passion and psychosis. It was like watching a live television show. I always feel like that when election season comes around. People start behaving so oddly. Anyway, I don't follow politics much, but when Chaka Fattah was caught up in scandals twenty or so years later, I wondered if Mrs. Johnson was sad about it.

Music was a big part of the culture of Emlen Elementary School. On a macroscopic level, I believe that the early '90s was a renaissance period for Black culture. I also believe a new cultural renaissance is underway as we speak.

Our morning announcements were brought in by Ray Charles singing "America the Beautiful" and Whitney Houston singing "The Star-Spangled Banner" on tracks through the loudspeaker, followed by our rendition of the Black National Anthem, "Lift Every Voice and Sing." We also had a drill team and color guard that we saw often perform outdoors on our "school spirit days," which was led by Mrs. Myers.

Mrs. Myers doubled as our lunch coordinator, so she was always on the scene before, during, and after the school day. She was a ball of energy, but she was also stern and strict. As lunch coordinator, she determined our recess time, so she had us on a string. Those minutes of recess time were precious, and who was dismissed first versus who had to wait meant everything.

But on days it rained or snowed outside, the lunch ladies would wheel in the TV carts and play Michael Jackson *Moonwalker.* The funny thing is, it was the only thing Mrs. Meyers ever played when we had to stay indoors, even if it was due to behavior. And every single time, she would dance along the lunch tables in full song just like it was the first time. It was fun to watch and almost made up for the fact that we couldn't play outside.

We had a glee club that I joined. Our music teacher taught us a song she had written called "Love, Peace, and Joy." It was about the *Fruit of the Spirit* (Galatians 5:22-23), which I related to bible studies mom-mom would have with me at home and the poster on her wall.

Me and my friend Jamar used to reminisce on how cool that song was all the time before he passed away in 2007. Jamar was "musically inclined," as he would say. In college, he climbed to become drum major of the marching band at Bowie State University.

So many of my reflections on the days of elementary and middle school were exchanged between us over the years. He had an impeccable memory of the details that elude most of us. Glee Club was certainly a safe space, and I found how much music relieves my anxiety and didn't give me a feeling of self-consciousness I felt doing most other group activities besides sports.

One thing that really pissed me off was not participating in the musical instrument program. I can't remember what it was called. I recall the wonder and excitement of touching and seeing all the instruments shown to us in our classroom for us to choose from. We learned the different musical groups and were allowed to sample some of the new instruments.

They explained how the instrument renting program worked, and we were sent home with permission slips. I chose to play the clarinet. It was bigger than the flute, and I liked the slightly solemn tone it resounded. I got home super excited to show my mom the paperwork and lock in this opportunity. But instead, I was met with indifference and a bunch of hemming and hauling, grunts, and shoulder shrugs.

I didn't understand what the problem was. When I asked my mom about her apprehension as she was reading over the permission slip, she replied, "I'm not going downtown to buy no reeds." My heart sank. I didn't understand her attitude.

I heard very well in school that the reeds were sold in packs and that it took a while to use them up, so her refusal to go buy the reeds, when the instrument itself was lent to me free of charge, was absurd to me. So, I watched my friends learn to read music and play flutes, violins, and trombones while I sat in the audience as they performed for us. It made me not even want to apply myself to anything after that.

I was always relieved that I was not questioned for not saluting the flag. When it was time for everyone to stand, face the American flag in the corner of the room and place our right hand over our heart to recite the Pledge of Allegiance, I sometimes would, but if I didn't feel like it, I didn't.

Mom-mom was a Jehovah's Witness, and saluting the flag was something (of many things) she put her foot down on. Mommy was not "in the truth," as they would say, but because it was mom-mom's rule, it was mom-mom's way. I'm not sure how many other decisions about my upbringing were entirely hers or were influenced or enforced by my grandmother.

There were many other directives for how to behave in school I recall being given. But the one I certainly wished that I had been given was how to speak up and stand up for myself. A healthy dose of confidence and self-esteem would have been helpful as well.

My classmates were clearly given directives on behaving and surviving in school. I knew because we were all repeating the things our parents taught us at home. "If somebody hits me, I hit them back," was often shouted aloud just before someone got socked. Maybe it was because I held my own so well at home, on Mayland Street.

Maybe my mom and grandmom did not even know the social turmoil I was in at school. I will always wonder why I wasn't given more tools to succeed, but I was purposefully indoctrinated to take a definitive stance on this one aspect of my school day (Hayes).

I did not know at the time the full political and historical implications of flag acknowledgment at that age. I knew for sure it was a deep-rooted situation, but I had no idea where I stood within it.

The end of third grade marked a maturity milestone for me. I had learned how to play spades over at my best friend Carla's house from her mom and aunt. Barry White's "Practice What You Preach" was on repeat in the background, and I felt like I was taking a step toward adulthood that weekend. I think we even snuck some liquor upstairs from her mom's dining room bar.

I also grew enough courage to draw a line in the sand and face my bullies. It seemed that overnight my fear of conflict had diminished. Facing disappointment and my personal desires being stifled, I didn't fear pain or defeat anymore.

My home and school social lives were starting to mimic one another, and I was beginning to feel squeezed. It was a feeling of disconnection from my parents arising within me. When my mother denied me a chance to learn to play an instrument, it disappointed me to the point of betrayal. How could she not see the mental stimulation and socialization that I needed so desperately at the time as clearly as I could? How could she have my best interest at heart and deny me this?

I knew a change was afoot. At home, when we all would play outside, the tides were changing from the younger years as well. Gone were the days of manhunt with the kids my age and older girls and boys all playing together. Things had changed. I recall the days being longer and the sun shining brighter back in the day. Everyone I mentioned this to thought I was crazy, but I vividly remembered the sun being so bright and yellow all day long that the leaves on the bushes would shine and glisten.

I probably remember this small detail of the sun due to the contrast between my school and home life and how it equated to freedom and happier moments spent outdoors.

Though we were changing, our school lessons remained the same. Science class was repetitive and remedial, but it was still classic, something familiar and close to me like the sun. We reviewed our five senses each year until the fourth grade.

And, periodically, our science teacher, Mrs. Bonds, would wheel in the TV cart and play movies for us. They were more like kiddie PSAs, but some were quite terrifying. I will never forget the one about dangerous gases. It was a low-budget production of people in assorted neon-colored, full-body suits playing the role of the gas. The radon dude was scary. He was scarier than the carbon monoxide guy who snuck up on that young, white couple watching a movie on the couch. So sad, they died.

The most poignant of all our science lessons over the years at Emlen Elementary were the ones about the environment. We learned of all the animals going extinct. We also learned that the world would eventually have so much pollution due to trees being destroyed and replaced by plastic, concrete buildings, and vehicles.

We were told that giant holes were being dug in the ground called land fields where all the trash was being dumped that would one day fill up. Over the years, that information caused us so much unease, and we all wondered what kind of anguish the future may hold and why no solution was given to us.

Our educators did not have a realistic answer for this impending doom, and my psyche was severely affected. We got the impression that we were being loosely informed because the problem would be transferred to us. They weren't even hiding it well, but the bell rang, and all the importance and attention of that subject was erased.

Chapter 2

Passin' Me By

"Used to catch us on the roof or behind the stairs I'm getting blitzed, and I reminisce on all the times we shared. Besides bumpin' and grindin' wasn't nothin' on our mind In time, we learned to live a life of crime"
- (Shakur)

4th & 5th Grade

After being severely picked on during the first four years of school, I eventually broke out of my shell. It all began on move-up day. That was the day at the end of the school year, after grades were in, where students learned what class we would be in the following school year.

This was an anxious, highly anticipated day for us. It would be on public display who would pass or fail that grade. It also gave us a glimpse of our new classroom's social environment. We were lined up according to our new room numbers and introduced to our new teachers at once.

My first observation of my new classroom was easy access to the lunchroom. This wasn't necessarily a perk. But I also realized there was a second class beside our class. I didn't see any of the girls who would bully me in either class. The relief I felt permeated my entire being and attitude over the summer going into the 4th grade. However, the reason for this separation remained a mystery to me until later in life. My classmates and I, some of whom are still my good friends and comrades to this day, shared and compared our experiences.

Once fourth grade was underway, I became far more vocal in school than ever before. It was much easier for me to socialize with my peers. Our classroom had a collapsible wall that divided our class from the fourth graders next door. Frequently the wall was removed, and we had class together, 50 to 60 of us. I don't remember one lesson learned that year.

My teacher, Mrs. Whitehead, was a very tall, middle-aged, overweight white woman. She had short brown hair and a slight limp when she walked. Our misbehavior often exacerbated her, and that was foreign to me. I knew older people were easily aggravated because my friends and I were constantly yelled at by our old neighbor Mr. Andy in the summertime on the block for playing too loudly.

But this was a new environment, vastly different from the home environment. I observed that people were generally more aggressive during school time than on the block. Although we fought at home, we intended to hurt one another for social gain at school.

The classroom design and decorum were very lax compared to K through 3rd grade. No bright-colored borders or trim along the box. Only the letters of the alphabet in print and cursive on a plain background. The teacher's greeting wasn't as warm in the morning, and it was clear she was ready to dismiss us long before 2:45 finally came.

Fights in class were frequent, and we were often too much to handle. In these times, our teacher would either send us to time-out or place us in another teacher's class to stand in the corner for a certain period, usually 30-60 minutes.

Our fights became competitions, live gladiator events for us. Through our confrontations, friendships and alliances were formed, and respect was earned among peers. My first-in-class fight that led to suspension was with my great friend today, Tina. We now have a business partnership and a podcast, and she is one of the photographers on this project.

The incident began when I overheard her conversing with a classmate sitting beside her. They were having a conversation about fighting, counting the girls in our class, judging if Tina could take them in a fight. When they got to my name, Tina exclaimed, "Lori! Oh, I can beat her easily. She ain't nothing but skin and bones."

In hindsight, we were nine or ten years old then. She must have picked up that expression from her mom and aunts. But her sass and sureness propelled me to jump out of my seat and backward, displacing our desks and knocking her glasses right off. She struck back mightily and rose up out of her seat to meet my blows. Before we realized it, our classmates from both rooms surrounded us and cheered.

Once our teacher was able to break through the crowd and toppled desks, a group of boys banded together and aided her in stopping the fight. She and I were removed and possibly suspended, but that does not matter in the grand scheme of things.

What matters is how everyone saw and remembered us from then on. Our fight was deemed a draw by our peers. Our abilities were on full display. I felt a sense of pride when people would bring up the fight. People looked at me differently and treated me with respect, most notably the boys. The memories of what took place that day have lasted throughout our lifetime.

We quickly lost respect for our teacher, and she slowly lost all semblance of control over our classroom. Her shouts across the classroom for us to quiet down had no effect. She resorted to snatching us by the arms and shaking us. Or grab one of our arms above the elbow and circle the classroom yanking us beside her uneven footsteps.

We would fight back and resist, but she overpowered us. When she was consumed with disciplining someone, some of us would sneak out of the classroom. I would go to the bathroom and meet up with my friend. We spent extended periods of time there unsupervised, doing all sorts of devious things. When we'd return, it was as if nothing happened, most times unnoticed.

I watched *The Simpsons* religiously, and I decided, one day, to try out this Bart Simpson line on my teacher I thought would crack everyone up. When she called on me for an answer, I said, "No shit, Sherlock." It went just as I imagined.

Towards the end of the day, when we saw our teacher was tired, we tried to push her over the limit. I remember her crying and pleading with us, but we didn't care. Looking back, I now find these memories of taking part in purposefully tormenting my teacher to be shameful and disturbing. At the same time, I found my voice in this environment and was accepted finally by the people whose opinions meant the most to me.

I didn't realize what we all had in common: we all had a hard time communicating. While some, like Tina and me, were known for being quiet, others were known for fighting all the time; and we were together. We weren't the "raise your hand" and "sit in the front" type. Nor were we the children who were strongly advocated for by our parents.

The principal never came to our class to back her or help enforce our teacher's integrity. It was as if we knew she was warden, and we knew she stood in between our freedom. We had been ranked and cast without our parent's knowledge. I mean, after all, there was no learning-disabled designation.

I think about how pervasive these prison-like dynamics are in classrooms throughout the country. Nothing in that environment fostered empathy. Our loyalty and camaraderie were stronger probably because we viewed our teacher as a common enemy. I'm sure her mental health was severely affected by our behavior daily. I can't imagine that was her desired career at that point. I wonder if she realized the cycle she was caught up in and if she was able to make it out.

1995

The summer entering 5th grade felt like the jubilee following the Emancipation Proclamation. The sun blazed down on Mayland Street, and our skin browned to our true hues with each growing day as the solstice extended our daylight. At school, move-up day once again proved to be eventful. After what seemed like a year in confinement, we were split up, reordered, and integrated back into population.

My newly formed fifth-grade class was a mix of funny and outgoing people who liked to create action but were not confrontational or mal intended; we were mainly out for a good time. Our new teacher was a dynamic, middle-aged Black woman with a commanding and regal presence named Mrs. Durham.

Her classroom looked lively yet mature, with plenty of wall décor and individually situated desks lined up perfectly facing forward to her polished, old-styled teachers' desk. It looked like an environment where individuality and curiosity could flourish, which I sorely needed from a classroom. Instead, a curveball was thrown our way, and I never spent one full day in Mrs. Durham's class.

Back home, there was an unexpected change afoot that altered my social life both at home and at school. I began to overhear conversations between my mom and grandmom about my dad soon after he came over to see me. It was quite uncomfortable getting used to saying the word "dad."

After the first visit, both my mom and grandmom immediately started coaching me on how important it is to say "dad" audibly and enthusiastically. After the next couple visits, they added to the spiel that "If you looked at his face, you could see the hurt in it, when I say bye", and left out the "dad" part. Over time, I came to look forward to my dad's visits, kissing his leathery cheek and watching him drive away in his pickup truck.

The appearance of my dad's pick-up truck on the block became a show-stopping event for my friends. Each time he turned onto my one-way street and was spotted, the sounds of people beatboxing *Sanford and Son's* theme song filled the street.

Soon I was running down the street followed by my friends to greet him, and he always came bearing gifts. Sweet watermelons, cantaloupes, and honeydew melons filled the bags he brought into the house. I eagerly ran inside behind him and watched my mom unbag the groceries and put them up. While watching, I awaited when my mom or grandmom would deem it ripe enough to cut.

With my dad's presence came an elevation in my social status. It wasn't just the fruit he brought that changed my lifestyle. He also helped my mom school shop that year. For the first time, I was able to get the shoes that I wanted to wear to school.

My mother did not go out of her way to make sure I was fashionable at school. I attribute a lot of the early days of being teased to that. On top of her not being a fashion first person in general, I believe her age had something to do with it. I observed that children with younger parents dressed far more stylishly than people I knew who had older parents.

The other obvious component is financial ability. And while my mother was not working, I'm sure other people that dressed nicely weren't more well off than me. And nicely does not mean name brand or most expensive necessarily. While I was always well-groomed, my mother did not believe in or see the value in buying things that she considered overpriced. But with my dad helping now, I had far more options to choose from and was confident I'd fit in the fifth grade.

The summer continued classically, and as I came of age, my interest in boys increased. The diminishing summer days before the school year began were a time of preparation. I was buying packs of hair extensions at the corner store when I saw a boy from school. It was Kyle from the fourth-grade class next door.

We had grown a distant bond since the day he helped break up the fight between me and Tina. At the store counter, he stood beside me and said, "Lori, right?"

"Yeah," I responded.

The cashier rang me up, and he said, "You're going to be in my class."

"Yeah, I am," I responded and handed the cashier my money.

"Alright, I guess I'll be seeing you around then," he said with a smile.

I got my change, took my bags, and walked out thinking that he just might like me.

The waning hour of daylight ushering in a warm, late August moon signified the approach of the autumn equinox. I began seeing Kyle around the way more ever since our encounter at the corner store. He must've watched me to see what street I lived on because he was around all the time all of a sudden, making friends with all my friends.

The summer ended with an epic game of "Truth or Dare" late in the evening on my friend's porch. After a few rounds and a few people were called inside for the night, the game got spicy. When my friend Robert was up, Kyle rose from his seat and whispered something in his ear that made Robert chuckle. When they were finished, both their eyes were on me. The dare was for Kyle to kiss me. We did, and when I went home that night, for the first time, thoughts of the first day of school gave me excitement instead of terror.

On the first day of school, my class was informed that Mrs. Durham would not be teaching our class. She was replaced by a new, 1st-year teacher Ms. Dyson. Her first point of emphasis was to not add an "r" to the "M-s" in her title because she is not yet married. Ms. Dyson was inexperienced, soft-spoken, and wore her hair in a bob like Regine from *Living Single* sometimes did.

We loved having a younger teacher, especially the boys. I'd see them cause disruptions on purpose in hopes of being moved to the desk she sat beside her reserved for troublemakers. They crawled under the desk and took her shoes off.

We fought in class. I made tickets for attendance to fights planned for afterschool in the schoolyard. Our disputes were usually over appearances and clothes, "busting contests" gone overboard. Luckily, I was able to get a few named brand shirts from the store thanks to my dad's input, so I was not a prime target.

Kyle became my boyfriend, and he was the class clown. His personality influenced me to be more outgoing than ever before. I was sent to time-out several times and learned the word *profanity* by seeing it circled on my time-out slip each time among the list of offenses.

At the end of the school year, my older sister Angie took me to The Wall, a music store, to reward me for my good report card. She bought me a CD for every A I earned. I had 3. I bought Busta Rhymes – "Woo Hah" single, Case ft. Foxy Brown – "Touch Me", "Tease Me" single, and the Mariah Carey – "Daydream" album.

Graduating from Emlen Elementary school and entering middle school led us all into the next phase of life and back down the totem pole of school seniority. The sense of ownership over your territory and social comforts are disrupted. But with the new presence of my father in my life and having a boyfriend, I felt confident moving on.

Children and Social Status

According to Dr. Bruce Lipton (Lipton), a developmental biologist, by the time we are seven years of age, the societal programming we all absorbed shaped our views of each other. You got bullied if your clothes were not labeled with a popular name brand. If your sweatpants did not have pockets, you were poor and teased all day for it. If you came to school ashy with a runny nose, that meant your mom didn't care about you and cruelly made you an open target for persistent harassment. We learned by observation, mimicking the beliefs and behaviors of all that surrounded us.

Moreover, we understood those social cues and beliefs to be "rules" that we assumed governed the world we were learning to live in. We weren't given the option to be coy. You will get toppled and starve. A closed mouth doesn't get fed, right? (That turn of phrase infuriates me). You couldn't show that you were too smart, or else you would get teased. Well, girls can be smart. That is expected.

But boys fair better having nice clothes rather than good behavior and top grades. Nice clothes are the top priority for both boys and girls. Loudness gets attention. Good humor is painful and personal. How should a girl behave, I wondered? How do I become cool? How do I get people to like me?

I learned that every social crowd is different. Some are no judgment zones, while others are dens of bullying and harassment. Sometimes the line gets blurred. I recall a golden time when there seemed to be an all-day orchestra of fun things to do outside. You might take your bike out early, ride for a while, break, then play some hand games. Then you might play red light, green light, or something like that. Then some freeze tag and run to the car and run back. By early evening you might play hide and seek and a game we called o'clock's.

My observations and experiences mirror what today's research validates. The socialization of boys vs. girls is different. What I experienced is that the boys and girls were slowly drifting apart as we got older. Playing as a group was less common, and I found myself playing house in the daytime and football at night. The interactions were different. With girls, our activities were more verbal and role play. With the boys, there was much more action and movement. But what I also found was that I felt more at home hanging with the boys.

Hanging with girls can be daunting if you don't have seniority or a speak-up-first attitude. With boys, there seemed to be less of a fight for acknowledgment. The rules of the game were what mattered most, and it was a meritocracy. An unlikely shot or catch can secure your place in people's minds and gain unwavering respect.

There were fewer chances to experience the glory of victory hanging with the girls. I realized that camaraderie was what I sought most and began to consciously cut out my all-female activities, including bringing my dolls outside and playing house. I enjoyed running and riding my bike much more, which girls were doing less and less of as we got older. Most importantly, I fell in love with the game of basketball.

I was not a part of the cool crowd at school. My friends were all outcasted from the popular ones. One of my closest friends was a girl named Charlotte. She had deformities in her hands and mouth because of her mom's drug addiction. Her younger brother's mental and emotional bodies were affected as well.

I would begin my walk home from school with her and hang out after school because her apartment complex had a playground. The three of us would have a great time. Her brother was an energetic and kind young boul[2]. He always had a smile on his face, and there was no judgment between any of us. No context to place any of our observations. We just played.

One day at school, I saw a familiar face walking beside me in the hallway in another class's line. My stare of trying to place her face in my mind caused her to look over at me. She was in a higher grade. She stared back with the same inquisitive look on her face, then she waved and smiled very familiarly, so I waved back.

I walked on, wondering what it would be like to be friends with her. Some people you come across, and there's something about their energy that makes you want to befriend them as if there was a connection between some of us that predate this life, a lasting bond that was forgotten then reintroduced.

While playing outside my house with my best friend from across the street, I saw three girls walking out of the house a couple of doors down from me. To my surprise, one was the same girl from the line at school. That is why her face was so familiar. I had forgotten a new family moved in two doors down from me. In time, as they got acquainted with the neighborhood, they took me under their wing. Our families got to know one another, and soon the girl I was staring at was walking me to school in place of my mom.

With them, I grew to discover that I love singing. We would spend hours singing with their karaoke machine, microphone in hand, speakers loud, usually playing Michael Jackson or Whitney Houston. Hearing their music had a way of breaking me out of my introverted shell. It still does to this day.

My rendition of "The Greatest Love of All" was one of my favorites and showed my vocal range in my mind. On top of singing, they were hilarious and extremely talented. One of their hobbies was muting the television and doing voiceovers of the scenes. They would also record commercials on a tape recorder; one was an infomercial and a customer testimonial about Spritz.

Over the years, as my mom and I struggled to keep my hair manageable, their interest and skill in hairstyling blossomed in line with my growing frustrations with trying to do my own hair. My mom was not a good hairstylist. That put me at a social disadvantage as a Black girl. I would envy the popular girls with beads and updated hairstyles weekly. In the back of my mind, I thought my hair was one of the reasons I was not accepted.

Katrina, the middle sister, practiced her braiding styles on me until she became proficient and then a master. The first set of extensions unraveled from the roots the next day. Practice made perfect; over time, she grew to be one of the best stylists in Philadelphia, and her younger sister followed.

Although I was not accepted by the popular crowd at school, having older friends helped me to learn how to express myself in ways I could not learn from playing with children my own age. And in time, as I grew into myself more, my ability to keep my hair up was a major factor in my elevating social status in school.

Middle school

After playing sports with the boys almost exclusively with all my spare time over the past few years, my athletic prowess developed. With my new love for the game of basketball came the summer Olympics and the NBA Draft of 1996. Penny Hardaway was my favorite player. I got his Olympic jersey as a graduation present and wore it with pride. Playing and watching basketball was the ultimate entertainment for me.

Watching March Madness, the NCAA tournament, with my family was always a fun occasion. I learned the nuances of the game from watching it with my mom, grandmom, brother, and sister. And I learned how to play the game in the streets from the old heads[3] on my block.

Philadelphia has one of the richest basketball legacies in the world. I loved the Orlando Magic, and The Sixers were secondary, but when The Sixers drafted Allen Iverson overnight, basketball went from a game to a lifestyle and the most important thing in my life.

On my block, we played basketball either with a crate tacked to a pole or a rock. The rock was an abandoned one-car driveway on the end of my block with a huge rock in front of the door we perfectly situated to be a basketball hoops width apart. There we played roughhouse and competed for hours, refining our skills. I was excited to play organized basketball for the first time and wanted to try out for the team in Middle school.

I attended Roosevelt Middle School. There were lots of kids from my elementary school here, but there were also a lot of new faces. The first day of middle school felt much like kindergarten. There was unsureness, except now a layer of self-consciousness was added. Like prison, we gravitated towards and banded with people from our elementary schools or blocks. There was a level of belonging and regard I felt between people I had a history with versus new people who seemed to be looking to mark territory to establish themselves as much as we were.

The environment was inherently competitive, and the 8th graders had a reputation for being great fighters. The fights at Roosevelt were bigger and far more frequent than in elementary school; they were old-school brawls. Mostly clean fights I participated in and witnessed, but sometimes people got rolled on.

Some seventh and eighth-grade girls took me under their wings and taught me how to slap box in the schoolyard. They also taught me how to carry a razor blade under my tongue, which I thought was so cool. I mastered the technique by practicing it daily. I felt like a member of Michael Jackson's crew on "Beat It."

My first confrontation was after a computer class. I sensed and heard trash-talking all around me the entire period, but I tuned it out. Talking to my friend Charlotte from Emlen was something I did every chance I got because she was such a funny person. She always had funny stories, and her commentary was entertaining as hell.

We were used to getting picked on in elementary school and had become good enough friends that we knew to ignore the bullshit and keep it moving when we were together. Then I kept hearing the words "gay" and "dyke" repeatedly said in the background. It was coming from a group of girls from another elementary school, and they were looking directly at us.

A light skin girl with long, wavy hair, referred to as Fefe, was leading the band of haters. That group was always especially rowdy and seemed to think they were the toughest. Charlotte wasn't a fighter. And they must have sensed that because they zeroed in on her. Fefe walked towards the trash can in front of the classroom, passed us, and pretended to accidentally bop Charlotte's head with her elbow. Infuriated, I stewed in my seat and plotted my get back.

I waited until class was dismissed and stood by the door, waiting for Fefe and her crew to exit. Before I knew it, a crowd surrounded us, and I felt a little unprepared for battle. We stood face to face and sized each other up; she was much shorter than me. I don't customarily wait to be struck first to ensue battle. But before I could plan my attack, she reached up and mugged me square in my forehead.

I retaliated by shoving her backward into her friends. It wasn't a punch like I wanted, but the shove was violent and sharp enough to whip her head forward and backward before she stumbled steps back into the crowd. Before either of us could attempt another strike, the next class made their way to the classroom forcing us all to disperse. I was unsure what effect that confrontation would have on my reputation.

I didn't particularly appreciate being called gay for two reasons: one, I did not believe that I was, and two, it was a huge insult in that day and time to be called gay. One friend was teased a lot by members of that same crew and was also called gay. When he came out in the summer, entering tenth grade a few years later, I wondered if their taunts influenced his orientation. When I realized I was gay entering my senior year in college, I wondered if they were social scientists or clairvoyant.

My dad began giving me an allowance which allowed me to buy snacks before and after school along with tapes, CDs, and magazines. That year, I had a legitimate Christmas. My mom and dad presented me with my first pair of Timberlands. They were big. And heavy as hell, but I felt so cool and couldn't wait to return from break. My dad painted my room, bought me jewelry, and a new Discman to play my music.

When I returned from winter break with my Timbs, on walking towards my locker, I left like I was receiving head nods and acknowledgments from people who didn't know me. After first period, while switching classes and groups of friends talking and passing one another, I spot Fefe and her crew in the crowd. I pretended not to notice them approaching me and waited from my locker for them to get closer.

When they reached my locker, Fefe leading the way, she slowed down, looked me up and down, and said, "Okay, Lori wit the Timbs. Comin' up in tha world." They continued down the hallway, and I sat there stunned, head cocked to the side, taking a moment at my locker.

After that day, I stopped hanging out with my friend Charlotte. My cherished bond since the early days was reduced to a wave when we made eye contact. After middle school, I never saw Charlotte again.

When spring arrived, we began having track meets. I trained with the older girls, who were all city runners. I had natural stamina, and I learned to run faster. Soon I was participating in 3-4 events every meet. My mom and dad only attended one game or meet I can think of. My sister was involved in my track career a lot.

The best part of being a student-athlete was the time out of class it afforded me. I feel like a lot of my personal development was due to not being confined to the classroom for eight hours each day. The discipline and teamwork that comes with attending practice daily after school also played a huge role in my mentality.

Chapter 3

School Daze

"These hot-headed youngsters always get into trouble Reactin' before thinkin' They easily irritated And murder's premeditated, it's a fact that we sinkin' When we should be climbing; in a nutshell, it's just jail Drug sales, liquor, and diamonds, niggas rewindin' Instead of moving forward, to blow up, so what's the science?"

- (Jones)

2000 High School

Entering high school was a culture shock for me, as is for most students. It did not hit me how few of my middle school classmates were going to the same school as me. In Philly, we had the chance to apply for admission into a public high school or flow into your neighborhood high school. Our chances of being accepted depended on our SAT-9 scores, report card grades, and behavior.

I got suspended all the time as I grew to love fighting and instigating fights. And I also loved being on the court and the track. Our track and field team was the best in the city for two of my three years on the team. We placed in the *Penn*

Relay's[4] and many of our girls went on to have successful track careers. Some of us stopped running in high school for different reasons, like me.

I played volleyball, thanks to Ms. Lowry, who was the coach and my gym teacher. She saw how my athletic prowess would translate to the volleyball court with my extraordinary leaping ability and quickness. I earned MVP honors in the only year I played.

I played basketball every day, and my skills improved over time. But my grades were average, and my behavior was far below that. I had cheated on my standardized test, and I wasn't even aware of my test results. The conversation I initiated at home about my high school aspirations did not give me any hope.

The school with the best track and field program in the city came to visit our school one day, and I told my mom that is where I wanted to apply. She said no, citing that the school was in a bad area. I attended a school that only had about five of my old friends and did not cultivate my athletic ability at all. I tuned out of school entirely.

I was so used to my mom not advocating for my education that I became apathetic. It was clear that Dobbins was not a good fit, but my ambition was scattered and waning. I never took the initiative to pursue a transfer. And at Dobbins, I didn't truly see a path for my athletic career; the school's sports programs were not highly ranked in the city.

School support waned for me in the upper grades as well. And the opportunities that Ms. Lowry exposed us to in women's sports didn't seem to be talked about anymore (much like the hole in the ozone layer). Besides, I thought, what's the point of playing women's college sports if it doesn't directly yield money afterward?

I did have a high school advisor, and he was a sweet older white man. He was responsible for the *Walt Whitman Scholarship* Program that rewarded honor roll students with money and bus tokens. He was an earnest man, but I had a hard time seeing any reflection of myself through him besides the spiritual limbo he was in, hoping to reach us. I related to the part of him that was drowning in his ideals without the tools handy to bring them into reality.

I lost myself in my music, TV shows, daydreaming life, and books. My sister Angie and mother are avid readers, and so was mom-mom. There was a great Black bookstore we used to go to all the time in Cheltenham Mall where you could find the latest in African American fiction from Omar Tyree, Terry McMillian, to Eric Jerome Dickey (RIP).

We had a routine of going there every other week or so and buying a few books each. She always screened my books to make sure they weren't too raunchy. But once I got a little older, she loosened the leash. At this age, I especially loved the romantic storylines and steamy visual sex scenes; so many ideas crossed my mind.

I was glad that she had given me more freedom because the world of Black literature was so vast. When *The Coldest Winter Ever* by Sister Souljah dropped, the hood went crazy. You could not catch a female on SEPTA[5] not sitting consumed by the pages of drama. I had never seen that many people reading.

Usually, people read the metro newspaper or maybe something else on the bus, especially the older folks. But *The Coldest Winter Ever* sparked a reading epidemic in my account. Dudes were reading that jawn[6]. That's something you just don't see every day around the way.

But as Angie delved deeper into Toni Morrison, slave narratives, and historical fiction, I found interest in Black nationalism. It was only a matter of time before I began to research the basis of the Tupac and Wu-Tang lyrics I was ingesting daily.

I also researched if Sister Souljah had written any more books. Turns out she had a prior autobiography. When I got my hands on that book, I read it, and my mind was completely blown. Never once had I been spoken to in such a direct and brutally honest manner, not in all my years of listening to hip hop and being alive on this earth, I never had. She somehow was answering questions I hadn't quite yet formed and foretold things I had not yet experienced.

On my next bookstore visit, I walked into the non-fiction section, looked at copies of T*he Autobiography of Malcolm X as told to Alex Haley* on the shelf, and told myself it was time to read this. It was a dramatic, traumatic, and pivotal point in my mental development. Internalizing life from Malcolm's eyes for 16 days changed me. I never looked at my life the same after that.

From that day on, I knew that it was my God-given duty to fight against the corruption of this system. I was angry and thirsty for more knowledge. I wanted to know the origins of the plight we have found ourselves in as a people, and I wanted to be an active participant in the revolution. I envisioned myself going from city to city, spreading the word of truth to enlighten people about their true potential. I ditched romantic novels altogether and delved completely into Black history.

When I turned 15, mom-mom told me I had to study and go to meetings consistently. There were three meetings each week, an hour of book study that was up the street, two-plus hours of Theocratic Ministry School, and the General Talk and Watchtower session at the Kingdom Hall, not including field service.

I was able to evade being too involved until now. She told me she was scheduling a weekly personal study with a sister from the congregation, and after a year, it was up to me to choose if I wanted to get baptized or not. I was appreciative of the liberty I had to attend when I wanted to up until then.

I loved my personal studies with my grandmother. Her love and knowledge of the Bible helped shape my mind and gave me ideas forming my first ponderings on my place in the world. But our lessons did not answer all the questions in my mind. I also did not have the vocabulary to form many of my questions yet. Therefore, I lost most debates with my grandmother.

But I was never a conformist; I often challenged the teachings. I remember debating the idea of everlasting life with her (Searcey). Jehovah's Witnesses believe that the earth will one day be restored to its original state of paradise. There will be people who survive Armageddon who will rejoin people who will be resurrected. Together we will grow into perfection, rebuild the world, and live forever, in everlasting life.

I objected to this idea at four or five, citing that I would not want to live eternity in the same state in the same world. I argued that I would grow bored. My grandmother reminded me that I'd be able to travel, explore, talk to, and be friends with animals.

But in my 4-year-old brain, a utopia seemed tiring. Later on in life, when the weekly study was mandated and enforced, I didn't tell her that I was researching afterward why we couldn't study from the King James Version of The Bible, despite her explanation.

My Uncle Ron always wanted my mom and grandmother to put me in modeling. As I developed into an athlete, he would observe me playing basketball around the house. I would sprint back and forth downstairs, then leap into the air practicing my arsenal of moves. He would call me a gazelle.

My mom was not in the business of taking the initiative, and my grandmother was a backseat driver. I did not take the modeling suggestion seriously despite Sarah, Katrina's older sister, saying the same thing for years. "Supermodel, of the world," she would yell out every time she saw me. "Lori's tall, thin frame, brown skin, and indigenous features are in!"

My uncle would brag from the living room, "She could be right in one of these magazines," holding up a fashion catalog.

Self-esteem was rarely spoken about directly in my house, but my mother indirectly taught me self-loathing. And there was such a thing as the "Chambers curse," which meant that bad luck and unfortunate outcomes are our fate. And that traits like running late and/or avoiding social interactions altogether were innate while also acknowledging that it often led to detrimental outcomes or missed opportunities.

I adopted the same attitude wholeheartedly until I discovered my passion in life, which gave me the strength to fight, but it remains a battle. My uncle's suggestions never went past that, but his unconventional and ambitious thinking stayed with me because it stuck out like a sore thumb within our family.

I am incredibly appreciative of the cast of people and community ties that led me to the path of college. Had it not been for my sister insisting and facilitating my attendance to the AKA and Alpha Phi Alpha Sponsored Black college tour in the 11th and 12th grades, I would not have pursued it.

God delivered me a mentor named Nadirah, who encouraged me to stay persistent at Clark Atlanta. Nadirah was introduced to me by my friend Alicia, with who I had been classmates since the 1st grade. Our relationship played a vital role in my transformation to actually pursue higher education.

I was not lacking ambition; however, hustling came quite naturally to me. I managed my income exceptionally well. I possessed a great work ethic and critical thinking skills. But I didn't see a clear and realistic plan for the next 10-20 years for myself.

There in my head loomed a constant ominous thought that I would not live beyond 28 years. That's where my daytime fantasy mental TV series leaves off, no official finale. There was no vision for my future, my prime, or my golden years.

Although only my best friend knew that I spent most of the day in my head daydreaming, I saw that the behaviors of my peers reflected the same mentality. We didn't really know what else to think of or do besides enjoy ourselves the best way we knew how and figure out how to make a lot of money after high school. We all were talented in some way at some point in our lives, but I saw the brightness dim in people's eyes around me over the years.

Some people were getting to a dollar as soon as elementary school. I remember our classmate Julius unzipped his book bag and showed us a bunch of weed and crack. In middle school, most of us started having sex; I certainly was.

By high school, some of my homies were poppin' pills. I was on the other side; I was an athlete. I was still starting for Dobbins' Girls Varsity Basketball team. And I still had a passion for running and football, so I didn't smoke at all. I only drank. Every time weed was presented to me in middle school, I scoffed and turned it down, stating, "I don't smoke; I'm an athlete."

But I really didn't see where my athletic career would take me. I learned from Love & Basketball that female ballplayers go play overseas for a decent living. There weren't many recruiters attending our games. The disdain and detachment grew to depression.

My school was not serving me. My family was not serving me until my sister intervened with the Black College Tour invitation. I felt my mother's attitude towards me was apathy and apprehension at that part of my life. My grandmother's devout Jehovah's Witness way of thinking didn't believe that college was a necessary step toward a successful life. Part of the reason my school was chosen was that it used to be a reputable vocational trade school. My father, a master plumber, saw an opportunity in that avenue for me.

My sister had attended college. But she was a straight-A, highly achieving student-athlete and attended the top public high school in Philly almost 15 years earlier.

However, the masses of poor Black children do not sustain high academic excellence throughout our school years, yet are geniuses like me. Most of us fizzle out once the content becomes difficult and class becomes more independently focused in the 3rd grade. That is around the time when the attitude of teachers is less friendly and more formal, and the classroom structure is less communal and supportive.

Most of the underserved masses are mentally and spiritually light-years ahead of the classroom matter and are not challenged and become disruptive in the box. I mean, classroom. Instead of being given the proper attention and assessment, then getting extra personalized material, projects, leadership, and social skills, we are left to our own devices or herded into learning-disabled classes. The system fails most of us.

Part 2

The Renaissance

Chapter 4

Higher Learning

"The superior man seeks neither a full stomach nor a comfortable dwelling place as his goals in life. He is quick in action and cautious in speech. He seeks the company of men of principle so that he himself may be reformed. Such a man can be called a true lover of learning."

-(*The Classical Library*)

Some of my fondest memories of the AUC[7] students are those times hanging out on the *promenade or the strip,* as non-Clark Atlanta University students referred to it (Consortium.). We would talk for hours, and school was fun for the first time ever. I truly was nurtured and poured into not just by the professors who were determined to see us all through but also by the built-in customs and culture and environmental upliftment of the African diaspora manifest.

In an uncanny twist of fate, one of my co-workers from the Popeye's chicken and biscuits I worked at in 12th grade had been accepted to Morehouse the same year I got into CAU, and wouldn't you know it, I ran into him, at our brother-sister dorm initiation. We had been reconnected.

Little did we know then that we'd develop a cherished lifelong friendship and help to transform each other into the best versions of ourselves through relentless debates fueled by our unquenchable passion for truth and justice. It was the love, the understanding, the laughs, and the wildly entertaining mindless banter that was so important to me. I learn life lessons from and through Julian to this day. Without certain friends, I just wouldn't be who I am today.

Hurricane Katrina

At the beginning of my junior year, Hurricane Katrina hit. Lots of relief efforts were promoted around campus, from MTV to Habitat for Humanity. My best friend Ebony was inspired to coordinate an independent student-sponsored relief mission during our spring break. We helped her raise over $10,000 and brought together a collection of 29 students from all three schools. A milestone was made for it signified unity among us when larger issues are at hand.

During times of peace, we'd have rivalries and an invisible social hierarchy, with my school being at the bottom. Despite the classism within our school communities, we successfully organized and executed our mission (despite our differences). Collectively we channeled the Black cultural legacy of excellence that had been held throughout the ages.

I endured a spiritual transformation in New Orleans. Our ancestors were invoked through us, for the pain of many injustices brewed up in my soul. Everything I had learned and witnessed up to this point seemed to hit me all at once. I had been led to my destiny, my mission for why I was born.

It wasn't legal maneuvers and laws that were the root of our collective issue. It rested in the beliefs and disbeliefs we have in ourselves and each other. It was education and economic power to establish culture-focused institutions that would reshape justice and our entire value system.

Finishing college was bittersweet. I completed what I set out to do. I didn't change course, and I did not quit. It was the most I could have said about myself up to that point. I knew that my major, English, was one of the toughest in the School of Arts.

I knew that my writing was strong at this point. My assignments had gone from the entire page written over in red ink, pointing out comma splices and incomplete thoughts, to my professors and academic advisor enjoying my content and encouraging me to continue writing because I seemed to have been "in the pocket." I knew that I had come a long way. But inside of myself, it didn't feel so. I still felt that somehow, I had failed, but why?

All my homies in Philly were damn proud of me. It was like we had all accomplished something. The way it should feel. But in my mind, I was behind. All my mates from the class of 2007 had moved on to careers from corporate America to Wall Street. A lot had gone into Teach for America, while others continued their studies in grad school. Everything that I stood for went against the process of making myself worthy by means of state evaluation.

I certainly was not willing to compromise my creativity and freedom by certifying to become a teacher, although teaching does provide a steady income for young professionals to start their life. It's a hard post-graduate path to pass up, especially with some teaching programs offering student loan forgiveness, and I accumulated over $100,000 over my five years.

My mission was to fulfill what God put in my heart to do in New Orleans, serving my people and not my personal security or comfort. Instead of pursuing a law degree, I had chosen a completely different path suited to my own lifestyle and the newly formed vision I saw for the future; I was back in my hood.

Chapter 5

Lessons on Leadership

"We don't need leaders. What we need is compassionate initiators and executors equipped with courage and faith. The Goal? An experience of independence and an overarching knowing of interconnectedness."

- (Lori)

At the onset of Finding Empowerment Through Education, I had no idea that I would end up operating it on my lonesome. But I guess it was foreshadowed from its inception. Me not graduating in the class of 2007 as scheduled sealed the deal. In hindsight, I don't know where I'd be if my life took the track of being on par with my peers at the outset of undergrad.

I struggled with comparison and compromise until I learned recently how to lead with me first in mind. It may seem selfish, but to an empathetic, people pleaser, it was a hard lesson to learn along the way. Not realizing at that time how imperative developing my self-worth was while working diligently to achieve individual and collective goals physically debilitated me over time.

Initially, it was a plan amongst a group of friends, or should I say super woke, young Black scholars. What I thought was a community turned out to only be a network. After everyone graduated and began the rest of their lives, I was left by myself to keep the idea going by showing the way to the next generation of AUC students.

It started with just me and John, who was a sophomore at Morehouse when we began. I was charged with replicating and expanding everything we had done as a group in the spring semester of 2007. We took turns teaching lessons we had created ourselves to our friend's fourth-grade classroom, blocks from the campuses.

The others worked out much of the logistics, and there was no blueprint left behind. All we knew was that we had completed a successful pilot. It was up to me to retranslate the lessons, find cohesion within them, and recruit students willing to volunteer enough hours to become competent in teaching them to a class of students.

I then had to build a rapport with a school's administration, propose a collaboration, have the ideas approved, determine a schedule, then coordinate volunteers to show up to the site consistently and facilitate a lesson for a group of children.

The pilot only consisted of the group who had conceived of the idea of teaching lessons close to their hearts. I was responsible for convincing people to give their time unpaid, to brainstorm and develop lessons as a group. I did not know if it could be done until I saw it blossom before my very eyes.

Armed with my Finding Empowerment Through Education/ Life Sciences Info Pack, I started my work. Soon I had a site, interested volunteers, and a seven-lesson skeleton course. My classes consisted of Maslow's Hierarchy of Needs[8], the color wheel, nutrition, active listening, music notation, note-taking, stress reduction and meditation, and foreign language and culture. The magnificent part that resulted was that the volunteers created half the lessons. Only two had been in the original pilot. The idea was taking shape.

People can come together to present a full learning experience to children without a state board certification. And the children loved and appreciated the material. I then began committees to help me manage the activity - recruitment, curriculum development, marketing, and fundraising. One of the most rewarding times in my life is seeing volunteers bringing new volunteers to our meetings already excited to help because they heard how rewarding the experience is, albeit hard work.

We were working on a shoestring budget. I used all my disposable income for classroom supplies. In theory, the graduating members of FETE were supposed to now be on a board of directors who would support the organization, obviously. But I did not receive a dime for operating the program from my comrades. My volunteers and I paid for any supplies we needed for our lessons, week to week.

We taught off an easel with a dry erase board, sometimes using a laptop and some speakers. Just like in the days of one-room schoolhouses, we made something from nothing. I never intended for a minimalistic environment to become part of the culture of FETE. It was just that I prioritized the urgency in getting the knowledge to the youth over what it looked like.

In the curriculum's transformation to New Element, I took full ownership of my mission. I intended to merge the best of what technology had to offer in safe dosages along with an authentic and natural methodology.

We continued forward with me at the helm. Some of my first volunteers moved up to lead committees, so I was able to focus on expansion. I connected with the school of psychology at Clark Atlanta University. I wanted my students to have access to clinical services. It is paramount in my philosophy to protect the child. The state of mind and the state of the home environment that the child is in has everything to do with his education. The classroom is all but a small part of life. I wrote a proposal to the dean for the help of interns with the then Life Sciences program.

It's my goal to cover the bases that prevent children from slipping through the cracks while strategically galvanizing all available resources. As far as I was concerned, I no longer needed the help or advisement of a board of directors. When members were able to come to town, they would come to visit the classes taking place. But the dream of us graduating and "getting crazy papes[9], getting paid from the devils" to fund our revolution was all but gone (B.I.G). But I didn't mind. I was going to do my work with or without them.

When I left campus for the day, I was either off to work or back home to my apartment. I did not have much of a social life at this stage. I mostly wrote notes and processed student assessments of lessons at home. I wrote concepts for school development and methodology. I did more than what a teacher is accountable for unpaid, for the love of the struggle. But I loved what I did and was completely satisfied. What seemed impossible was now my lifestyle.

I realized that the same mentality I applied to hustling could be applied to directing education programs. Materials, timing, preparation, a pitch, producing consistently, and customer-centered experiences. I also integrated my work experience in fast food, call centers, catering, coaching, and now Life, Accident, and Health Insurance.

Once I moved to Philly at the end of 2011, I was in search of like-minded individuals, although I thought FETE, as I knew it, was gone without my original base of volunteers and money. I had fallen on hard times and lost everything because I thought I had found love with the wrong person. I ended up in many compromising situations I didn't think I'd find myself in and had totally lost myself.

One day I was at City Hall reading a book I purchased from Black and Nobel Bookstore and was interrupted by an elder with locks taunting, "What do you know about Heru?" We struck up a conversation and exchanged numbers. He told me he was a member of the UNIA (Universal Negro Improvement Association), Marcus Garvey's organization. When he said that, I was stunned.

I had no idea there were still any active chapters because I would have found them and joined by then. He told me he hosted a radio show and was looking for young people to contribute to removing the generation gap. He said he had another young sister in mind that he wanted me to meet and that he'd have her contact me. "Her name is Shanita!" he exclaimed. I was elated to have met him and took that as a divine sign that my work would continue in my hometown.

Operating an organization within a college campus is totally different than doing it in the city. There are libraries and places to host meetings in a city, but there's not a central location. I'm from Germantown, and I found myself still without a steady income and no car, which isn't unusual for a Philadelphian.

We have one of the largest public transportation systems in the country, but it still doesn't make it sweet.

The sista that the elder introduced me to contacted me almost immediately and was interested in hitting the ground running. I walked from my crib off Tulpehocken and Baynton Street to Brickyard almost daily and made trips to North Philly and West Philly multiple times a week.

There were different collectives with their own lanes putting in work, some involving community gardening, politics, veganism, art, and music. Nothing existed that I knew of that related to education and entrepreneurship, so I proposed FETE at a meeting of the minds one day.

People really took to the idea, and before I knew it, my childhood friend, Shanita, and three others were all in on the idea of educating the youth of Philadelphia. This is where my leadership skills would really be put to the test. It's fairly simple to manage college students. We already adhered to a daily schedule, had the same general life goals, and were the same approximate age.

Everything was centralized, and the volume of the noise of the world was adjusted circumstantially. In Philly, it was a completely different ball game when it came to managing people, not so much their actions but their desires. I learned to listen to people's ideas while also declining them. I also had to learn that my millennial collaborative approach to getting tasks done was not the way for my vision to be carried out properly.

I ran into many issues by not repeating the same processes I used in Atlanta. I had built a successful model for the organization that lasted four solid years, including one full year of FETE's smooth operation where I directed my volunteers remotely when I had to move back home after losing housing in Atlanta temporarily. I am unsure if my processes were impractical to duplicate or if I just sacrificed order and the proper structure I worked so hard to build because I wanted to appease my new collective. But it began in error.

Instead of letting the structure grow organically as it had in Atlanta, I immediately handed out titles and divided the labor into roles, with no clear chain of command. Thinking that I was a proficient delegator and judge of character was my downfall. I found that it was hard to make decisions because each of us had differing, equally important jobs. It was like one delegation stating concerns to the other and me in the middle. I did not establish an adequate hierarchy, so there was no way to weigh one objection over the other.

So, to keep everyone happy, I made compromises. I held extended meetings with lengthy discussions trying to arrive at resolutions, only to have my own desired outcome muddled and distorted along the way. The result was more talk than action, a reality I never wanted for myself.

It was a great time for professional development in both practice and philosophy. I extended my curriculum and tested its flexibility in even more environments than before. In 2013, I launched my first Home School pilot.

I learned so much from the experience, the full potential of the then Life Sciences curriculum with the proper funding and personnel. But also, something less apparent is the variety of ways in which children are raised and that role in forming their attitudes towards children's preparedness in structured learning environments.

I also learned that leadership is more about giving clear direction when communicating and constantly evaluating your alignment with your inner compass. It is quite easy to veer off course and waste time backtracking when too much diplomacy is involved with radical change.

I prefer to work singularly and then present the plan laid out. Those of integrity and diligence will last, and those full of rhetoric will not. The agent provocateurs will be spotted, and all evildoers will be sniffed and eradicated.

In my new vision of leadership, I intend to overcome a lot of the scenarios that stopped worthy movements from continuing. I am not looking for a group of people who think the exact same way, forming a fake and exclusive community. We all have roles to play, the churchgoer and the drug dealer. When we work in unison, we can bring forth our own personal power.

An article on Chron - small business states that "ideally, team diversity is composed of the six major personality types. Different personalities can motivate one another, while similar personalities may prove to be detrimental in a workplace environment" (McFarlin).

Our victory is our destiny. If we apply innovation to business practices and galvanize and harness the brilliance of our youth together, this current generation can help make a better future.

I am designing a curriculum and looking to build learning spaces in places all over the world for people who never before had access. There is content within all of us yet to be presented to the world that will change the fate of a seemingly dreary future right in favor of the impoverished and unrepresented in this current system.

The great wealth transfer is here, and it is up to us to "Cast down our buckets where we are" and transform the world around us through thought and action. We are all leaders of our own destiny.

Chapter 6

The Audacity is Within You to Teach

"Tell the children the truth"
-(*Wailers*)

My deep conviction is that my experience and subsequent insights are the only qualifications needed to consider myself a subject matter expert on this topic of education. It is an audacious assumption that I will take to the grave that it is my God-given mission and birthright to translate, transfer and add on to helpful solutions for our life's problems and correction of the abuses against nature and humanity.

I am no more extraordinary or gifted than anyone. We all have God-given talents and strengths. The quote, "Your calling is where your talents and passions intersect to meet the needs of your people," became my mantra and lifestyle. What I created was a world in my mind first. One that I would feel free and comfortable, yet still stimulating and personalized. Through my persevering through 18 years of school, at age 22, I began to integrate all my teachings into a curriculum that I could share with anyone in need of insight.

The spiritual teaching I learned from my grandmother was now more relevant than ever. After studying many religions and spiritual systems, I found the vein of truth within them all. I integrated my study of revolution, and I found peace within all the wisdom of the examples left by our foremothers and fathers. I no longer viewed the philosophies of Dr. Martin Luther King and El-Hajj Malik El Shabazz (Malcolm X) as oppositional any longer. I put a lot of effort into cultivating my spiritual discernment, and, in turn, my mind was open to new concepts. I applied the foundational principles of the Black culture that raised me to my recreation of education, Hip Hop.

As program director, I constantly labored through state and national curriculum standards to formulate the methodology for the lessons we taught each week. Our goal was to enrich and enhance traditional content while introducing lessons outside the scope of normal schooling. The second component is how I designed the learning environment; that idea spawned organically.

I am revolutionizing education. As Black people, a part of our culture is re-learning and unlearning, clarifying, reinforcing, etc. No one can stand between us from using our minds to teach another what we know. Damn the classroom from this day forward. You are the teacher where you stand. If music taught me anything, you are both the instrument and musician. You are the DJ and the producer who creates your own masterpiece in time.

The DJ is the foundational element of hip hop. That individual is all a master of social science, sound, and vibration. The architect of the song is a musical historian finding the perfect break in a song to loop. This oscillation, repetition, or rhythm is a call to the spirit within us that resonates with harmony.

The DJ is also a doctor, assessing their patients' ailments (the crowd/audience/ people around) and prescribing medicine in the form of music. The transmutation of energy performed by the DJ, taking something old and making it new, anticipating, and observing the chemical reaction within another human being, is alchemy. The call and response of our music are genetically hard-wired into our DNA. I consider myself and the ideas I bring forth the ***New Element.***

I used my experience in school as a template for how I would like things to be done differently. Just as a DJ/producer reviews many records in search of components to a new masterpiece, I first identified what was useful and what needed to go within the education system. Some things are fundamental to the educational experience and are productive habits or values to have taught in school. Realizing the extent of what I did not know about myself and the world around me was astonishing and angering and shaped my personality.

But I am not a reformist. I believe in eventual 100% community/family funded and operated, culturally relevant, historically accurate, empowering, nurturing, and fluid, personal-centered education for all children and adults across the board.

We are not taught to be individuals. Our minds are not trained at any point to look within to find our inner passions. Moreover, we are conditioned to deafen our inner voices, which should guide us over the voices of society and caretakers in an effort to civilize us.

But more importantly, the deconstruction of self with the tools that I now had gained in college left me in dismay. Why were there so many things to life and myself that I simply did not know? Why was certain information made to seem so complicated to the point some others were afraid they wouldn't understand?

A former teacher and author, John Taylor Gatto, stated in his book, Dumbing Us Down, "If I do my job well, the kids can't even imagine themselves somewhere else because I've shown them how to envy and fear the better classes and how to have contempt for the dumb classes. That is the real lesson of any rigged competition like school. You come to know your place"

Gatto's point is that the compulsory public school system suppresses our sense of curiosity and ambition at an early age. Furthermore, our minds are deluged with negative expectations, which are essentially curses on our young lives.

Curriculum

Throughout my studies at CAU, it occurred to me that my personal, educational journey was systematically segmented and inverted. This means a child's mind is at its highest absorbency and peak curiosity. It is dumbed down by outdated, dominant cultural beliefs. But here is the ruse, the beliefs were given to us by media and institutions of power, and the power that represents them is not held by themselves.

For instance, although we all know better, the dominant belief is that babies come into the world ignorant and have to be taught the alphabet and numbers first in life. I would argue that some would say reciting a prayer to a child would be more helpful. I guess the question comes down to what we intend to become and who intends this for us. The education provided to children of privilege is the opposite education that is given to children who are intended to stay poor, plain and simple.

I began composing this curriculum every day in my notebook, on the ground observing and talking with people in the city. I talked to young bouls selling drugs on the block and the old heads in the parks and partnered with a pastor of the community. We all want the same things but lack the way and means to bring them about. We lack the faith that others see what we see. That is the one thing I want to impart to you, the audacity to be effective.

How I transferred these philosophies to facilitate the New Element curriculum began with my definition of self. We believe many things told to us that we don't have the audacity to challenge. Our education is why we are angry and confused. By the time we reach adulthood, we are used to being defined.

I encourage all who answer the call for a transformation to first consider themselves a teacher and a student. As a teacher, I have to be accountable for the nourishment I provide. As a student, I must relearn the very idea of imagination all over from the perspective of my child self.

Foundational concepts of New Element

Distinction and scope of the New Element curriculum and university retreats as it compares to traditional school/education centers.

The initial goal transitioned from helping youth within public school systems to a model that will provide a more well-rounded education and add value to the behavior of learning. Spanning the last decade, our New Element curriculum covered topics relevant to personal and community development, mathematics, communication, cultural heritage, global languages and perspective, leadership, self-expression and esteem, natural sciences, and social awareness. We worked with youth ages two through eighteen years of age.

Now I seek to expand our scope to accommodate dropouts, home schools, children with special needs, group homes and other juvenile facilities, English as a Second Language, people living with disabilities, and other marginalized populations in the United States. We begin as early as six weeks of age and continue for all adults. My curriculum development volunteers were always the backbone of the program in its early implementations. Now that department will continue to build the foundation and will eventually consist largely of early childhood educators, psychologists, and researchers working on effective models for each stage of development.

The self-designed curriculum, which is called New Element, has been our niche in the youth education sector. The mission of FETE is to eliminate the social and economic restraints resulting from a lack of education. That is why the continuance facilitation and dissemination of the New Element curriculum is paramount to the future of education in America and the survival of our communities.

We are looking to reform people's attitudes and behaviors towards education. I want to make this fun and user-friendly for parents. One issue with online school and homeschooling is that parents are either out of practice or are unsure of how to teach their children the curriculums given to them. With school closures across 188 countries (as of April 2020), many parents are exploring alternative ways to provide continuous education using technologies such as live and streamed online classes. However, access to these technologies is limited and ineffective in many low and middle-income countries, especially among poor households. (data.unicef.org/topic/education/covid-19/)

I plan to reach students in a more accessible and approachable way than the current public-school model can afford or cares to offer. We will completely transform the value and meaning most of our national places on education. The classification and predetermination of children through the public school system is made possible through indoctrination pushed by media and well-meaning parents who follow the direction of supposed leaders and laws in hopes of a brighter future for the underclass; hopes never fulfilled.

The education system suppresses the people from true information, and we are therefore unable to unlock true personal freedom. The insidious nature of our miseducation as a mass through compulsory schooling was not fully evident until such apathy and permeating anti-intellectual and non-life-sustaining behaviors began to manifest in our children and in the streets in the forms of drug epidemics, mental health breakdowns, and heinous acts of violence.

I believe that people subconsciously know they're being lied to and react in various ways. It has not done us as a people a service to believe that we can achieve whatever we want because our realities don't reflect that. And because the nagging inarticulable feeling of being lied to has no satisfaction, there lies an urge to dismantle what is known to be true and sacred.

According to David Stovall, professor of education policy at the University of Illinois at Chicago, "it's critical to guide young people from "defiant resistance" – defying what they learned to be untrue regarding a just and fair system for all to "transformative resistance" – developing a critical understanding of the historical context of U.S. society." Stovall is warning that teachers and parents must not play along with the fairy tale that we live in a just society because in doing so, we risk losing our children to the streets.

According to the article, Why the Myth of Meritocracy Hurts Kids of Color by Melinda D. Anderson, new studies find that believing society is fair can lead disadvantaged adolescents to act out and engage in risky behavior (Anderson).

The essence of this study corroborates what I assert: people are out here knowing we don't have an equal playing field. However, there is no peace in knowing without having the power to act; and there lies our inner conflict. FETE's New Element curriculum will empower our children with the truth.

We traded a seat at the table for our children's minds, and for it, our families are even more impoverished as inflation, ignorance, and competition soar. We used to share neighborhoods with one another, providing and receiving most of our services while holding the mentality of shared triumph and struggle. With the invitation to join from white corporate America came conditional inclusion and incentive for individual pursuit.

Commenting on this aspect of her work in the essay "Love as the Practice of Freedom" from her book Outlaw Culture: Resisting Representations, bell hooks wrote, "When masses of black folks started thinking solely in terms of "us and them," internalizing the value system of white supremacist capitalist patriarchy, blind spots developed, the capacity for empathy needed for the building of community was diminished (hooks)." In other words, bell hooks believed that for individual achievement came the sacrifice of community values, which robbed us of our identity and self-determination individually and collectively.

Observing our environments, we can see that communication is obsolete and that intolerable behavior is left unchecked and unaddressed by our day-to-day duties. How FETE and the New Element concept contribute to changing trends in today's communities is by shifting the traditional approach to an all-encompassing education by creating an education publishing company that houses not only a full-scale curriculum but also integrates entertainment, social and human services to be delivered to youth and adults in person and by digital, video media.

Create Your Reality – Control Ourselves – New Element!

Part 3

The Regeneration

Chapter 7

The Dilemma in Teaching Black History

"Take me to another place, take me to another land. Make me forget all that hurts me, let me understand your plan "
-(Development)

Highlighting important accomplishments of Black people does not erase the gaping holes in our access to accurate information as citizens of the world.

Let's search within ourselves to apply radical thinking to reshape our collective life experience. Let's stop teaching our children that racism and greed are innate within white people before we teach them about mind, body, spirit, and nature.

While awareness of racism is prudent for self-preservation, we don't realize how limiting that mindset is in that it robs us of our power to create our reality. We erroneously accept all negative circumstances as facts of reality, thus leaving us helpless in seeing the congruence between our thoughts and the actions within our lives.

If we want to continue recounting a Middle Passage narrative, then we'll always be slaves, and if we want to only focus on successful Black insurrections and ancient kingdoms, we continue to further ignore the observations and applications of that information to emancipate us today. If things are constantly evolving, our mindsets have to evolve as well.

Everything we know about the world is told to us from the perspective of our oppressor. We do not know the true nature of anything, history, geography, etc. Therefore, we uphold our great Black scholars with the highest esteem to break through to the masses, delivering information that was only speculated or never even conceived of before. We know it's true because it not only resonates within us but is naturally symmetrical and empirical. As much as we have accumulated individual accolades as Black people, we have not solved a central problem in our pilgrimage to emancipation in this country; we do not control our own information.

How can we continue to feel downtrodden by hopeless statistics about ourselves that are not even verified? People assume that numbers do not lie, but the way they are presented and the factors of calculation damn sure can be deceiving. To advance in our struggle for self-determination as people, we must heal our hearts. I believe it is the reason why we relive the trauma of our history instead of applying the hard-learned lessons to the future.

The mind is suppressed if the heart isn't free, and the same is true in reverse. The truth is that the history books studied throughout the United States have been written and distributed by the conqueror for generations and are therefore criminally inaccurate and psychologically devastating. There is a place and time for certain dialogues within a child's development.

We are searching for Maat[10], the balance, justice, and middle ground from what we all have learned from experience. History is vitally important to forming one's identity and, therefore, a determining factor in sustained success and the transference of generational wealth.

Parental practices are as diverse as this melting pot of a nation. The implementation of parental styles can be on extreme ends of the spectrum. For instance, the side leaning to the far left adopts the principle of allowing the child the liberty to dictate every aspect of life. The parents on the far-right abuse their authority by enforcing unattainable guidelines in the name of control and orders while using fear of emotional detachment and excessive physical force to garner obedience in children.

Instead, we are looking to cultivate a feeling of safety and belonging within every child through a pedagogy centered around an appreciation for nature. We intend to develop a steadfast and resilient attitude and spirit in each student while also cultivating a critical and curious mind throughout the youth of this generation and the ones to follow.

A hard fact to accept for the Black community is that we attach too much to outdated mindsets and practices. What worked then doesn't necessarily work now, as any snippy teenager will remind you. But this is true in most instances in life. Therefore, it is hard for the Black community to still share common values. We all have chosen to move differently based on our past experiences. Individually we each internalize life uniquely, so it stands to reason that we have all made choices to ensure our survival and personal comfortability going forward.

In 2022 in the United States, integration has been successfully completed. There are more bi-racial and multi-racial American Citizens than there are ones that can claim to be full-blooded of one group or another. Many Black nationalists, which I consider myself, still believe in separatism. If I'm not mistaken, a lot of far-right Americans feel they want to return to the separate but equal golden years of old. But the fact of the matter remains, the American melting pot is oozing over as the population expands and more and more children have to live with the realities of two opposing historical and cultural heritages being within them.

The solution for racism is no longer separatism. I propose we update, correct, and narrate our own history as honestly and instinctually as possible. We are the new historians. We are here to tell the truth about indigenous people worldwide; we are ubiquitous throughout the world like the soil. We are the composition of the earth, each cell charged by the spirit of God, contained and sustained by the water around and within us.

In the age of technology, we have witnessed information processing leap light-years in front of our very eyes. Where the most studious of us would nestle up beside a good ole Encyclopedia Britannica in the mid-'90s to take in information, now internet browsers and YouTube videos can build one's confidence to proficiency level without having stepped one actual day in the field researched.

Something about the gravity and girth of an Encyclopedia reminded you that you are a student and that mastery is a lifelong journey, a humility that today's media simply lacks. But if we applied the confidence today's formal, or should I say informal, way of imparting knowledge gives us, we should be doing much more with our so-called "know-how."

My mission is to impart that whatever your area of interest is in life, you can ignite interest in someone else in that area; that is Black progress.

For a child, whose main objective is to train and study during childhood for what kind of adult they want to be, we must be willing to face our children and give them accounts of our lives without the adversary's ability to misconstrue and intercept your expression. We need to be the heroes, role models, and authorities in our children's lives, each of us, those with and even without children.

Most celebrities are fake, an illusion, a figment of our imagination. Gone are the days of old, now only a few true ones can shine, but most have been converted into actors and agents, even our most beloved. I salute those of you who are out there serving as leaders of your communities both formally and informally.

What Makes FETE Essential to the future?

There is an array of African center curriculum packages available on the market today. Some brothers and sisters are focusing on STEM subjects and formulating math and science curriculum. Others are introducing our children to Black history events and figures while building their esteem and confidence, while others place emphasis on financial literacy. I am proud of all these people bringing the knowledge forward.

I believe the key component we are missing is culture. What links our various experiences? It is our interactions with one another. It is the ability to make our individual experience a shared one. That is what the power of music does. Elders have tried to integrate uplifting values into music, but it often comes off corny.

What we are demanding from ourselves is to produce content that is not only empowering but is also trendy. It is time for the expanse of the Black community, from millionaires to corner boys, to come together to raise the value of our content.

We need the funds to write our history as it unfolds and to collect and redistribute our own resources amongst ourselves. Relying on information and assistance from anything but true allies has held us back for too long.

In the right hands, technology and social media can solve our issues of the day. Once we force ourselves to divorce the programming fed to us about where our community is going, it will allow us to reflect on our own ability to affect change around us. It is possible for us all to begin to make changes where we are and then share that experience with one another.

It is possible for the person who has the resources to help the person who does not but is in the position to physically be present, to work together. That is the New Element–FETE is bringing to Black culture. There are logistical issues that can be easily solved if we trust one another. Some of us are going to have to be brave enough to want to change.

From the comfort of our homes, we can create content to change the world, and we can safely come together. Social interaction and communion with nature are human requirements, and we will not allow fear to suffocate us. With FETE bringing forth knowledge and hope through the countless outlets we have available currently, we possess the power to determine the quality of our lives. All things are possible through our Creator and our obedience to that source in our hearts and minds. There is an alternative to doom and madness. We must create it by stepping into our God-given right as co-creators of our lives and destroying all the enemy's projections.

Employing Youth Teachers

We are the solution. We developed a youth teaching division of New Element, a system for youth to refine their knowledge and leadership. The "student-teacher" will be able to refine knowledge taught to them in their previous grades while working on their public speaking and leadership skills and use the experience as a preparatory lesson valuable to any future endeavor.

The outstanding students in our program will earn teaching positions and deliver lessons to children two grades lower. We will really have young people teach other young people by having 12th graders teach 10th graders, 10th graders teach 8th graders, 8th graders teach 6th graders, 6th graders teach 4th graders, 4th graders teach 2nd graders, and 2nd graders teach Kindergarteners.

This will allow young people not only the opportunity to be able to teach their younger peers, but there will be other benefits to it as well. The "student-teacher" can progress through the program and earn the qualification to teach by being an outstanding student in their grade. FETE will negotiate the terms of each student's class credits and accommodations, including, but not limited to, time of service. School teachers will also serve as an additional reference for student strengths building a network of accountability and supervision for student teachers.

FETE Academic Research Board

Many people think that because certain seemly obvious social ills have not yet been corrected, they cannot be corrected. Some of this is due to us not knowing our rights. Some of it is due to the observation of our complacency. Rarely are the renegades highlighted. Our enemy will not hand us over the gamebook, or review his defeats with us, so we will not get reminders via mainstream media, but he does have a knack for writing everything down. Some of you have the same ambition as I do.

At first, I wanted to see a school, then a school district. I studied successful models of neighborhoods being transformed and longed for that sort of success to expand. But where is OUR national board of researchers analyzing the successes and failures of our projects and initiatives? Where is the data that allows us to crunch numbers and learn what works and does not work for our community? What is true and what is just made-up propaganda to discourage future attempts?

As much as I hear each time I watch the news that Black people are more susceptible to this or suffer more from that, I wonder, how the hell would we know for sure? Who that represents Black people is back there checking the math? The Black employees who work for these corporations, universities, and international cartels are no help. They're contractually obligated to represent the company's interest in exchange for their livelihoods.

I am left to believe a lot of things are bullshit built to eat away at our self-esteem and self-perception. Why do we accept being told negative things about who we are instead of researching and highlighting extraordinary things about ourselves?

But when a Black person talks about melanin, they're being a reverse racist or not inclusive to all?! Mental slavery, I see it as. If our collective conscious perceives our future as being sickly and grim, why do we wonder why we kill each other so easily? "You cannot hate the roots of a tree and not hate the tree," Malcolm X said. By the same token, you can't hate the outcome of your life without hating your life. And that was the inexpressible depression I lived with until arriving at college.

I could not even conceive of the anger within me. I somehow sensed that everyone was complicit in it but could not pinpoint how. My anger was in our community's seemingly inability to think big enough. I was afraid to think big enough for a very long time, still thinking it was my role in life to be humble, modest, and meek; good Jehovah's Witness characteristics.

I was told by a colleague from Philly who spent time in California that I had an idea that could change the world. But because I was so distrusting and lowly, I didn't even see my ideas translating to a mass audience. Now, this is the time. I would have no idea if I had the confidence sooner what the outcome would have been. But I am grateful to still be here with the same passion hoping that we can help one another out in some small way.

"Until lions have historians, the tale of the hunt will continue to glorify the hunter."
-African Proverb

A research board with our brightest analytical minds equipped with the latest in information processing technology could change the scope of the community. The social revolution I dream of is bridging the gap between our academics, fully embracing them, and inviting their presence to our table. The child's mind and heart would wake up within all of us if we were allowed to ask the unanswered questions swirling in our minds. In an age where facts are debated and the scientific method is unheard of, we must step up as explorers in our own lives.

FETE serves the needs of the people. When we establish an academic branch that rivals the current establishment by cultivating our youth and then enlisting our Black minds into earning a living by solving our problems, we could see a transformation in life as we know it. This information can then feed current curriculums and make an accurate, relevant, and people-backed curriculum, creating a new national standard for all moving forward. It is time for us to pick up our crowns and clean up our kingdom. The world is ours.

What Sets My Redevelopment of FETE Apart from Other Initiatives?

What sets FETE apart from other organizations is my scope of service. I am creating a new academic authority that feeds culture and curriculum development worldwide. The revolutionary aspect of this idea is that by forming a for-profit education-focused publishing company, as opposed to a nonprofit education foundation, as we initially began, we will have the protection of our intellectual property and the ability to redistribute our content created together. We can develop our ideas as a collective and make it our mission to distribute our lessons to any child, educator, youth organization, or individual wanting access.

Children worldwide can learn on the same accord and interact with one another electronically, on FETE campuses, and in community initiatives. Sometimes it takes a different voice for a message to be heard. Moreover, the distribution of content will generate revenue. Generational and community revenue will come through publishing, where an otherwise voiceless individual may now have the chance to be heard. An artist's broken dream of fame may be mended by their stories heard, maybe not via a major record label, but perhaps through a new screenplay, book, or lecture distributed around the world.

Instead of Making Children College Ready, I Intend on Making College Optional.

The potential economic impact of an established publishing company serving the interest of the Black community worldwide is massive. We can create a system to identify new writers, develop and produce content, and choose the terms of redistribution. That means that an individual, by sharing their idea with FETE, could release a published work to the public and receive residual income indefinitely. The lessons can be taught for a lifetime by all who choose to participate. It all begins with an idea. But why me, you may ask? Because it must be done. Let's do it!

Our minds, energy, and bodies fuel the world we live in. Yet we as a people have little ownership and little control of the institutions, companies, and systems we dedicate ourselves to in exchange for our livelihood. It is time to bridge the gap between Black businessmen and women and the disenfranchised and underserved of us. We are all one life. However, the system feeds off separating us from one another in ideology and in our fashion of getting to a dollar to support ourselves. We, therefore, cast judgment on one another.

I have lived in several Black communities throughout Philly, where the residents' household incomes, compositions, and values differ. Sometimes, you'll see the scary folks whispering about the activities of the young people at the end of the block. The folk might even be neighborhood watch or got the cops on speed dial just in case a nigga would.

But how many of these folks do you see reaching out or establishing a better way of life, healthy outlets, or streams of income for the young people? The few who do are heroes who need to be celebrated, protected, and upheld, not celebrities who leech off their former hood affiliation long after selling out to the elite's agenda.

We are no longer standing for this sort of behavior in the community. I will follow through on the plan FETE is extending to the people to RE (prefix: again, anew) MEMBER (noun: one of the individuals composing a group of our community). We will have quality resources, services, and education in our communities. That is the leadership I've never witnessed before.

Chapter 8

New School

"It is clear, therefore, that we do not have in the life of the Negro today a large number of persons who have been benefited by either of the systems about which we have quarreled so long (education and economics)."
-(Woodson)

The public education systems throughout this nation, especially in cities, are more like holding cells than learning environments. Also, however, for a child, the home can be a prison. I did not personally experience this, as my household consisted of three people for most of my childhood. And fortunately, I did not ever experience a move that would interrupt my schooling.

Although I did not experience my home being a prison, I did experience a significant household transition when we added my niece to the family. These factors alone can have long-term effects on your self-identity as well as your ability to perform to school system academic and behavioral standards. The children who needed the most support at school likely had more responsibilities and less parental support at home due to socioeconomic circumstances.

We consider it progress to see economic strides in the classroom like e-texts and laptops because we thought that was what our inner-city schools were lacking to produce high-achieving students who would become productive and successful adults. But this is false. It is also false that attending college guarantees subsequent economic success. Most people do not know that wealthy children do not get the same education as poor children. And there is no reason why we should continue to accept a substandard quality of life when our survival depends on it. Real progress can happen, and it will happen.

Sometimes it seems to escape the poverty cycle, Black children must become athletes and entertainers because half of the college-educated individuals have nothing to show for it. But often, we do not consider the parental dedication it takes to develop and support a top athletic prospect. If only our community heralded other professions with the godship of a star basketball player, could we redirect our teaching to supporting a person's genius in whatever that may be? This behavior, over time, may eliminate the need to play the economic Russian roulette (financial gamble) on a college education. This shift in culture requires family and community reinforcement and can only be done by individuals in their own minds and hearts.

Reclaim Community and Childhood

I am not a parent, so I'm reluctant to speak about managing life with a child, but I am an advocate for both parents and children. This movement is about hearing the needs of today's parents and creating resources and services to make bringing a healthy child up manageable in today's world. We have abandoned the old cultural credo, "It takes a village to raise a child," right before my eyes. From the '90s to the 2000's I saw our community whitewashed with the individualistic mentality of, "You better not say anything to my child." The irony is that I found that many mothers with that fight first mindset in the street about their children are often neglectful.

As a result of the individualistic mindset of our community, a lot of our children have fallen through the cracks. Following the coronavirus outbreak and the national school shut down, I had to dig deep within and make myself available to parents and children seeking a stable and sure future.

I cannot stand by the wayside while others are suffering from an upheaval of life as they knew it. I don't believe there has been a time in American history when children have been home 24/7. But I know for some, it was not healthy for the child's development or the parent's sanity.

We must learn how to set aside our differences. Whether you're pro-vaccination or anti, raw vegan or carnivore, East Coast Muslim, or Southern Christian. The fact of the matter is that until we can sit down at a table and break bread across the board, our children will continue to suffer because of egos that are being fed.

Continuing down the path we're on will lead to the extinction of the Black community. Religious, political, and dietary differences cause the masses to fight one another for the scraps while big corporations merge and powerful nations form alliances. We are being led astray.

If anyone in power who claimed interest in the issues we face really cared, there would be more support and empowerment of the parents, who are gatekeeps to the future, our youth, but are themselves trapped in the prison of political corruption, economic and time limitations, and failed social policies. Who provides the provisions, commands, tone, and aesthetic of our world? Why do we allow ourselves and our families to suffer alone to be uncared for, for so long? Who is to blame, us or the system?

Why are teachers so severely underpaid in some districts that some people can slip into the system and masquerade as educators while they snatch the souls of our children eight hours at a time? Since when was teaching a hustle and not a passion? How did the schoolteacher position get relegated to a high-stress, high turnover industry with the power equal to that of a babysitter instead of an ordained guide of self-mastery?

I believe this system gets the exact results that it wants from this way of doing things. It splinters the minds of Black communities and set-in motion probable life outcomes that favor the few and not the collective majority. They want to produce distracted, defeated consumers.

We, as adults and parents, are left working long, grueling, and consistent hours to work our way to a comfortable management position in some corporation, a city job to enforce systems and policies (with no ability to affect or profit from the machine), or entertainment. For most, college begins with debt.

Trade schools are a wonderful option, but they do not develop the person as a whole, which I can say Clark Atlanta University successfully did. For a smaller financial risk than college, a trade school will teach you a skill that will allow you to be qualified for a high-wage career path and offer the flexibility of working independently and becoming an entrepreneur. However, what it doesn't do is directly help you foster a relationship with the community.

My mother and father meant well when they suggested that I attend Dobbins. But we are no longer living in the era where our schools offer anything worth much of a damn due to budget cuts. They didn't realize sending me to Dobbins would not give me a skill I could use to earn a living. I spend my shop class time playing Tetris. What they failed to do was proactively parent.

They may have assumed that I was a "set it and forget it" type of child, a self-starting achiever who can excel without steering, oversight, or much guidance. But I don't see those children often. Most of us, if anything, need extra attention. And there was no excuse for the lack of guidance as there were no siblings remotely close to me in age. It was based on the fact that they did not know me as an individual and did not engage in my school life.

Many poor Black parents have a misconstrued notion of the role school plays in life. That is the primary issue I have with the attitude toward education in the Black community; I believe it is linked to the desire to integrate and assimilate. I was not alive in the '50s, but I heard the stories, and I witnessed the devolving of the generations.

Sistah Souljah states, "The parents of the Black children were confused as well. Either they were overworked and undereducated (thus uninvolved in the schooling of their children), or they were Black professionals interested in advancing in the white business world, assuming to be successful they had to accept and even celebrate white culture as their children did in the advanced classes."

In making this comment, Sistah Souljah urges us that we should strongly consider the decision to assimilate to the pace and expectations of today's world to provide a better life for our children, for we risk losing touch with our children.

Affirmative action and higher education are different discussions altogether in terms of the furthering splintering of the Black community. Still, in terms of the scope of service the school provided when we were in one-room schoolhouses with just a few tattered texts to circulate, it was clear. The relationship of the parent to the teacher was totally different from what it is displayed largely today.

Parents today that I observe expect the teacher to educate the child on all matters of academics. As a result, most have taken their foot off the pedal as primary educators in their child's life to just being providers. The first years of a child's life are the undisputed primary learning ground. The home, good or bad, is where all things are internalized. Some parents are not equipped to create a proper learning environment at home because they expect the school system to evolve with the current days and times we live in.

With most of us adults, male and female, working at a minimum of forty-plus hours a week, commuting, shopping, cleaning, maintaining, organizing, and socializing, you wouldn't even think there is time in life for distractions, but they are there. With the endless streaming services and programming being released at what seems like a faster pace than the increase of automobiles, we are getting around-the-clock alerts for breaking news, scandals, crime, viral videos, and other pressing content that must be ingested to keep up with water cooler discussion.

Our own personal brands and social media life are now integrated with our homes and private lives like an automatic transmission in our cars. It's extremely difficult to spend time with oneself nowadays, so when it comes down to family time and one on one time with children, even with the time set aside and the proper intentions, how easy is it for our minds to truly provide undivided attention to someone, especially our children?

The renowned inventor Nikola Tesla agrees in his book released in the year 1919 when he writes, "The pressure of occupation and the incessant stream of impressions pouring into our consciousness through all the gateways of knowledge make modern existence hazardous in many ways. Most persons are so absorbed in the contemplation of the outside world that they are wholly oblivious to what is passing on within themselves."

In other words, Tesla believed over 100 years ago that life's demands pulled us away from sitting with ourselves and further stressed introspection as the key to success. Can you think of how many more distractions we have in life than the people who lived in the time of the telegrams and oil lamps?

Gadgets and technology equally seduce us. What game consoles, cell phones, and tablets are today are what the TV set was for some of us in the past; it could be a conduit for family time and boding or a place keeper for actual quality time.

We are suffering tremendously emotionally and mentally. Failing to take accountability for the atrocity women as parents and primary caregivers have played in our generational trauma and how that has manifested into the degradation of our culture is living in denial. We are building schools the way you've never seen them. There will be an alternative to ongoing child neglect and broken government systems.

Homework

We need a culture and environment that invites reward and upholds and promotes learning. I've seen homework create tension and resentment in family bonds rather than build them. Instead, the child will initiate his/her own environment by actively taking part in their education plan. The tools gained from school sessions will be practiced at home, and New Element will provide resources.

Solve practical problems

Nowadays, in the essence of time, we are limited in family time, so we do the best we can to compensate with additional gifts, games, and activities. But nothing compares to undivided attention. Even as adults, when we are alone, do we even have our own undivided attention most of the time? Several reports have come out in recent years stating the idea of multi-tasking is a myth. With the understanding of mindfulness becoming more prevalent, it is my hope for the future that we as a collective innovate in the areas of social efficiency and continuity between the school, home, and surrounding community/village.

We must assess the entirety of our problems as Black people in America and use our mathematical and creative skills to solve this issue of time in our lives. We need to accept that modern life is too hectic and overwhelming for any of us to take on without help. For us to successfully and usefully navigate as individuals, we need the help of others. There is no way around it. We all fall short in some categories, but we are stronger together.

I gained enough field knowledge through my facilitation of FETE from 2007 to 2013 to not only see the ills of the school structure firsthand but also of the home, hood, and social construct. Although the compulsory school curriculum is shitty and has left out vital ingredients in making a complete person, we must take accountability for the mentalities we adopt into our culture.

The bullying I faced in school was included to highlight how the same mentality we have towards one another as adults are played out amongst children. The haves and have-nots exist in every social circle, be it a classroom, a country, or a group of five friends meeting up. It is within our capability to shift that mentality and teach another way to children.

Before the government ordered schools to be closed, our community schools were already at their breaking point, and many parents had opted to home school their children. Now more than ever, we need each other to put the pieces back together and establish a new normal that is comfortable and healthy for both parent and student. The most noteworthy dynamic I observed in my homeschool pilot between the parents and children was an unhealthy emotional attachment established and continued by the parent.

The sensitivity and censorship the parent imposes on a learning environment can sometimes be detrimental to the child's development and hinder independent thinking and behavior. If I could do it all over again, I'd establish a healthy boundary during times of instruction. Simply put, mothers who prefer the homeschool option often hawk over their children and are overprotective to the point of being a handicap to the child's development.

We are all simply too busy, and it is okay. This is an indictment on society and not the individual. But in doing so, I am not abdicating the personal responsibility of each parent to prioritize and take the lead and follow through in their child's education. But ironically, taking the lead that I implore from parents today involved setting aside the ego and, in a way, surrendering the control and allowing a new approach to be introduced that I intend on presenting.

Paradigm Shift

I propose a complete overhaul of the current national curriculum. But what I am seeking even more is a complete paradigm shift in how we, who are not rich and privileged, look at education. And that goes beyond any new, African-centered individual educational tools. I believe the entire path from K-12 through college should be redesigned, and that is just what New Element does.

We need men and women of integrity and righteous intent to unify. First, FETE will seek out existing and developing youth programs and services with shared values to form new cultural solidarity. Through uniting our efforts to educate our community, we will create new avenues of access and resources. Most importantly, communication and connection never before seen in this era will be possible.

Individuals who have long fought for similar causes but remained members of different groups will have the opportunity to work alongside one another and realize common ground. The knowledge and wisdom circulated through us are what regenerates our wealth.

Yes, I said regenerate what once was to create generational wealth for your family. If we do so, the next generation will have a completely different experience of life that we all wished for. But that change does not come from laws and policies. It comes from the hearts and actions of people. It is up to us who recognize the problem and then work on creating an environment that provides a solution.

Let's generate change, and I guarantee all will follow. We just have never been shown a way. The consciousness within you has been searching for a realistic, practical solution to act on. We have been misled by wolves in sheep's clothing for too long.

We are afraid to approach one another, so we teach our children not to trust one another. This mentality has left us to depend on our enemy for food, clothing, and shelter rather than one another. We have a litany of Black businesses manifesting before our very eyes, and we continue to grow individually. But we do not have a central vehicle in which to harness our energy as a collective. I am afraid the fate of our newly established businesses lies in the attitudes of us, the consumers, just as much as it does, the entrepreneurs.

As consumers, we must stop asking for discounts. I am glad we are in this new age of awareness and audacity that I see more entrepreneurs receiving the full price for their products and services from friends and family. Businesswomen and men must hold themselves to the same expectation that you must deliver your good or service consistently and indiscriminately. The way you would treat a client of high influence is how you must treat your cousin. Because we as Black people talk so much, we cannot afford to circulate negative customer service experiences.

Secondly, we must circulate our funds and resources amongst ourselves more. People who are members of congregations benefit from that community's support, but the rest of the Black community does not operate that way. We are a patriot of the company that cuts our checks. Most of us are not affiliated with a church that will help with rent or have connections to local jobs or mosques with an inner gifting system. The fake communities we exist in now don't bring us closer to independence or inner peace.

We must circulate our resources while establishing the trust that comes intrinsically with religious affiliation. Trust grows from the sacred spiritual bonds we forge through the exchange. We, the people, are the congregation, the black sheep who have been making our way and growing more fed up with the course we are on.

Even the financially free of us are not free because we see the neighborhoods we love and grew up in chaos. We feel a tinge of guilt every time we clock in and adhere to those company policies instead of finding a way to help. But how? Are all the problems in the Black community too bad for one leader above us to overcome? Without spiritual intervention, the answer is yes.

Plan of Action

Economic Change is in How we Educate and Empower our Children

This concept invites our current Black and Brown businesses to form a network that allows students to a. apprentice, b. gain employment, c. obtain partial ownership. FETE will serve to cultivate the relationship between the economic potential of the Black community in a strategic way to deprogram ourselves and our children from a generational poverty curse.

This is achieved through hands-on financial education spanning from customer service to accounting. The problem is that many Black businesses simply lack resources, and our youth are equipped to fill those positions and keep quality businesses viable.

That initiative is a tremendous stride for economic sustainability. The path for youth will be:

1. Education in business administration.
2. Opportunities to develop/implement business plans for business network participants.
3. Apprenticeship to acquire key operational knowledge.
4. Transition to partial ownership.
5. Financial security for a family.

The benefits for Business owners in the FETE network

1. An extension of the business's lifespan by injecting new youthful perspectives on its operation,
2. leading to increased customer traffic and sales conversions.
3. Implementation of efficiency-driven technology and practices to sustain business quality.
4. Additional staff which allows for a less rigorous workday and partial retirement
5. Leaving a legacy with your name, knowledge, and wisdom carrying on.

The power of the oppressors could not last forever, and we now have a plan of action on how to resurrect ourselves. If we all sustain our paths individually, our collected victory is inevitable.

This initiative would also reinforce the attitude that patron accountability is necessary for all small businesses, especially Black businesses, to survive. We all know shitty service is shitty service no matter Black or white, but why do we as Black folk feel that tinge of guilt right after we complain about how poorly a well-meaning, Black-operated business is run? I believe it's because our inner self knows that interaction causes a ripple effect across the tide of Black trust. If Black trust is broken publicly, how can any one of us vouch for anyone outside of who we can personally account for?

Bad Black business is what set-in motion and continues to sour the perception of consumers like you and me. Things like, why are these prices dramatically higher than the white competitor? Why is the service taking so long to be delivered? Are people lacking courtesy and etiquette and doing things they wouldn't do if masa were around? Real questions we have all asked ourselves at some point, in one form or another over the years, as we all are observers of life.

I genuinely believe we are leaving the days of bad Black business behind and entering a new elevation of mind, spirit, and matter; we are forming a New Element. So, FETE takes the responsibility of becoming a change maker in this area.

Classism in the Black Community Creates Subdivisions

There is a definite class line drawn in the Black community between those who have graduated from college and those who haven't. We internalize the details of our personal educational outcomes, often both consciously and unconsciously. When we are at work comparing our current position amongst coworkers with our education, we often see vast variations in the paths that lead to the same point.

When I was a life insurance agent just finishing my undergraduate studies, I was the new kid on the block; young, gifted, and Black. Other people chose to enter the field because it did not require a college education yet yields one of the highest returns of any sales industry in America. Others had been in entirely different fields for years, be it in engineering or corporate management, before realizing the financial independence and potential in insurance independent sales.

In short, the array of life insurance agents you'll meet is just as varied as the talents and skills we have in the Black community. We all had different backgrounds yet pursued the same career at the same time at different points in our lives. We do not tend to compute that the same is true of us and our diversity as a people.

Therefore, with optimal utilization of our collective resources and a new paradigm of education for the next generation, we can make higher education a part of the everyday Black experience instead of a place only a few get to experience.

Chapter 9

A Different World

"Any movement that can effectively address these needs of the spirit in the context of liberation struggle will succeed."
– (hooks)

We, as a collective, have reached a breaking point. White and Black alike have been too dependent on government and corporations to sustain our livelihoods. The dramatic fashion in which the nation was shut down in March of 2020 was jolting to every American's psyche. The rat race stopped for the first time; schools and jobs shut down.

People knew it was really getting real when professional sports paused. Life was in chaos for some. The stillness was peace for others, a reminder that we all reside in different worlds. Children home twenty-four hours a day is a new precedent in American history. We are in a position to RECREATE our culture, our idea of how education coincides with day-to-day living, and revalue our community currency from the inside out.

Once again, right in front of our eyes, another public execution of a Black man, George Floyd. With the anger and angst brewing against the justice system, the spiritual abuses of patriarchy, policing, and white male dominance in general, our emotions, white and Black alike, spilled out onto the streets in the form of looting and destruction nationwide.

The White House was stormed by people who disputed the legitimacy of the presidential election being won by Joe Biden. Others have hated Donald Trump and all his supporters for years. In the age of information, there is more division, illusion, and deception than ever. Critical thinking and spiritual discernment are key to navigating society peacefully yet firmly.

Some had built their hopes and dreams around America's promise with the full faith and assurance that this country is strong enough to withstand itself, only to learn now the security blankets were as thin as mist.

The disharmonious state of the world fuels every crime against humanity and nature that we commit. It is the souls yearning for more, realizing each thing we were robbed of one by one, cutting us deep within.

The sharp contrast between what I was learning in K-12 vs. all the cool information college was exposing made me rethink how deep the sabotage went. I didn't know whether to consider myself lucky to have knowledge because it felt more like alienation. To know that I was given empowering messages to a degree, within that extremely critical time in brain and social development, while knowing that so few Black children get a chance to go to college and stay in college for the duration, is deemed a human rights atrocity in my book.

Our minds are purposefully set against learning and engaging critically with our inner and outer environments due to the deliberate programming we receive in our early years of education. Usually, by the time we're adults, most of us can't completely unravel the puzzle of ourselves because our minds are distracted and oversaturated with endless mundane tasks, breaking news, celebrity scandal, and government upheaval, not to mention the personal and immediate duties, crises, debt, and ongoing developments, time, and unforeseen occurrences.

The academic disparity between poor minorities and those with means and ownership is closing. This is the beginning of a new era in the culture of the oppressed worldwide. Our images of struggle and beauty are what keep the world entertained. Our minds create the best we have seen. Our countless hours of labor built and upkeep every system, industry, and institution we fall under. We are the power, and we shall inherit the earth. This is when we realize the only things of value are ourselves and the nature around us that allows us to exist.

What will New Element look like? I envision establishing Research, Resource, and Retreat centers focused on the needs of our people. We will form new channels for our goods and service to produce revenue and employment for our community. We will create new school campuses that don't resemble correction facilities but are rather retreats for children and young adults to go and experience peace, safety, love, and compassion. Sharing the teaching of Shambala warriors in her book, World As Lover; World as Self, a scholar of Buddhism Joanna Macy writes, "You have to have compassion because it gives you the juice, the power, the passion to move. When you open to the pain of the world, you move, you act."

"But that weapon is not enough. It can burn you out, so you need the other—you need insight into the radical interdependence of all phenomena. With that wisdom, you know that it is not a battle between good guys and bad guys, but that the line between good and evil runs through the landscape of every human heart. With insight into our profound interrelatedness, you know that actions undertaken with pure intent have repercussions throughout the web of life, beyond what you can measure or discern." Macy is affirming our need for one another for success.

There are among us individuals desiring to unite and uplift our communities. With your goal comes discouragement at times from allies and adversaries along the way and moments where things seem hopeless. Our problems can seem insurmountable, for they come in all forms and are both internal and external. If you do not know where to begin, start from within. "Put on the full armor of God, so that you can take your stand against the devil's schemes. For our struggle is not against flesh and blood, but against the rulers, against the authorities, against the powers of this dark world and against the spiritual forces of evil in the heavenly realms. Therefore put on the full armor of God, so that when the day of evil comes, you may be able to stand your ground, and after you have done everything, to stand" (Ephesians 6:11-13).

Each of us reuniting with the God within is the only way to achieve inner peace and become a changemaker. This is the game I have learned over the years. My only hope is to pass along the things that were told and taught to me that stuck out as pieces to the puzzle.

This is a time for healing and for coming together. With our collective might and whit, we can create new systems that support our needs and place our children's protection at the forefront. This is a call to action in the face of social anxiety and fear. This is a call to action in the face of alienation and past failures. I am looking for contributors to this initiative. I am looking for people who desire change to come together.

My view has been partially formulated by early Jehovah's Witness indoctrination, years of research thereafter, and constant reflection. The doctrine of a New System never left my mind as I expanded my knowledge over time. Recently emerging theories within quantum physics, which I have been studying for some time, gave me hope and confirmed my determination to translate my information to the masses and invite you to shape a new reality along with me. The only thing real in this world is the intangible self within. In bell hook's view, "Without love, our efforts to liberate ourselves and our world community from oppression and exploitation are doomed". Hook's point is that LOVE is the invisible cord connecting God within us to all things projected outside us.

That is why I am one of the most dangerous people on this planet, a Black child who grew to maturity; capable of executing our greatest elders' and ancestors' hopes, dreams, and plans.

There is more. There is a spiritual transformation taking place. Some people call it an awakening. We are seeing through the illusions and finding our truth within. Whether Black or white, our culture has always been to define our lives for ourselves. There is enough space for us all to rebuild ourselves first, circles, and then our communities in order to sustain ourselves. We must remember ourselves. We must save our children.

Acknowledgments

First, I thank God almighty for grace, mercy, love, and inspiration. Without the love and grace God has shown to me over the years, I would not be here standing and breathing in courage.

I want to thank my parents, who allowed me to and created me to be one of a kind. Mommy, thank you for reading to me and never judging me for being peculiar. Dad, thank you for sailing with me and being a life raft in this journey of life and allowing me to be yours.

Thank you to my partner and soulmate, Chi. I love you and thank you for supporting me every step of the way in the process of making this book. I am eternally grateful to be sharing this life with you.

To my brother Neil who taught me that there is more to life than what meets the eye. Thank you for cultivating the music historian in me by constantly remarking, "What'chu know about that," every time I attempted to sing along to a song that came out before 1985.

To my sister Angie, thank you for bringing me up. I really can't say enough about my brother and sister. They are 10 and 14 years older than me, respectively; they practically raised me! Thank you, Neil, for making sure I read and knew Assata Shakur when you saw that I was waking up. And finally, Neil, thanks for burning all those Stevie Wonder CDs for me in chronological order and giving them to me in intervals.

To my niece, Kayla, thank you for always being in my corner and understanding me from day one.

I thank God for the gift of friendship that has given me priceless wealth in this lifetime.

To my homies, Mark, Julian, Ebony, Mooro, Shawntina, Tina, Alicia, Chris, Earl, Sherae, Danny, Ase, and Libby, thank you for the countless hours of building on revolution into the wee hours of the morning, support over the years, and for you, all becoming and helping me become the rightful heirs to our divine crown.

I want to thank Chanel for inspiring me to write this book, mentoring me, and bringing me into the BTBM family. To my elders who took me in and gave me love, Denise Ford, Charmayne Thompson, and Priscilla Dames, Tina Marie Coley and James R. Benton Jr.

Thank you to those who are not here anymore in this form but guide my inspiration, Benjamin Pressley III (Hubby), Jamar Smith and Nadir Chambers, I miss you every day. Mom-mom thanks for your wisdom and the protection you gave me.

Keturah Caesar, you took me in as a little sister the first time we met. Thank you for your loving and energetic spirit, your tremendous outpouring of light shined on all our hoods and the children, and all the time you spent bringing integrity and goddess-ship to the movement.

And to Nas (Nyier Parkour Cunningham) ande Mikey, two beautiful spirits that transitioned while writing this book. Mom-mom thanks you for the wisdom and the protection you gave me.

Thank you to my extended family and friends from Mayland Street.

Works Cited

- n.d. https://whatis.techtarget.com/definition/Maslows-hierarchy-of-needs.

- Anderson, Melinda D. "Why the Myth of Meritocracy Hurts Black Kids." 27 July 2017: 9.

- B.I.G, Notorious. "Hope you Niggas Sleep." By Christopher Wallace. 1999.

- Brown v. Board of Education of Topeka. No. 347 U.S, 483. United States Supreme Court. 17 May 1954.

- Consortium., Atlanta University Center. aucenter.edu/about-us/mission-vision/. 2021. <https://aucenter.edu/about-us/mission-vision/>.

- Contributor, TechTarget. "Maslow's hierarchy of needs." April 2019. https://whatis.techtarget.com/definition/Maslows-hierarchy-of-needs. 16 2 2022.

- data.unicef.org/topic/education/covid-19/. "Education and COVID-19." 2020.

- Development, Arrested. "Tennessee." 3 Years, 5 months & 2 days in the Life Of... Atlanta, 1992.

- Ephesians 6:11-13. The Bible, New International Version, n.d.
- "Galatians 5:22-23." Version, King James. The Bible. https://www.biblegateway.com/, n.d.
- Gatto, John Taylor. Gatto, John Taylor. Dumbing us Down: The Hidden Curriculum of Compulsory Schooling. Gabriola Island: New Society Publishers, 2017. 4-7.
- Hayes, Liz. A Timely Celebration Of A 75-Year-Old Supreme Court Decision Protecting Freedom Of Speech And Religion. 23 October 2018. <https://www.au.org/blogs/wall-of-separation/a-timely-celebration-of-a-75-year-old-supreme-court-decision-protecting>.
- hooks, bell. Outlaw Culture: Resisting Representations. London: Taylor & Francis Ltd, 2006.
- https://en.wikipedia.org/wiki/TGIF_(TV_programming_block). 1 January 2022. online. 16 February 2022.
- Jones, Nasir. "Purple." The Lost Tapes. Long Island, 2002.
- Leasnam. Wiktionary.org. 30 March 2020. 3 April 2022.
- Lipton, Bruce. Biology of Belief–Part 1 of 2. London Real. 10 September 2017.

- Macy, Joanna. World As Lover; World As Self. Parallax Press, 1991.
- "Marita's Bargain "All my Friends Now Are From Kipp.." Gladwell, Malcolm. Outliers. New York City: Bay Back Books/Little, Brown and Company/ Hachette Book Group, 2008. 250-269.
- McFarlin, Kate. "Importance of Different Personalities in a Workplace." n.d. SmallBusiness.com. <www.smallbusiness.chron.com>.
- Native American Boarding Schools. Dir. Indigenous Americans. 2019.
- Owens, Cassie. "Bol? Bull! Why we can't agree on how Philly spells slang." The Inquirer 31 August 2018.
- Reeves, Dianne. "Better Days." DianneDianne Reeves. Hollywood, 1987.
- Searcey, Dionne. "People Would Be So Receptive Right Now, and We Can't Knock on Doors.'" New York Times 19 April 2020: 6.
- septa.org/about. 2022. 3 April 2022.
- Shakur, Tupac. "I Ain't Mad at Cha." All Eyes of Me. 1996, 1996.

- Shakur, Tupac. The whole world leeches off the hood MTV. 1994.
- Sheep, Black. "The Choice is Yours." 1991.
- Souljah, Sister. No Disrespect. New York: Vintage Books, 1994.
- Tesla, Nikola. My Inventions. New York City: Electrical Magzine, 1919.
- Wailers, Bob Marley & The. "Babylon System." Kingston, 1979.
- Woodson, Carter G. "The Mis-Education of The Negro." The Associated Publishers, 1933.
- The Classical Library. 2001. 12 July 2022.

End Notes

1. TGIF is the name of an American prime time television programming block that has aired on ABC at various points since the late 1980s (https://en.wikipedia.org/wiki/TGIF_(TV_programming_block).

2. Philly slang: pronoun, informal - A person who is either younger than you or is smaller than you (Owens).

3. (African American Vernacular) An older person, especially one who acts as a leader or mentor (Leasnam).

4. The nation's oldest and largest track meet, held annually at the University of Pennsylvania. It was one of the few major events that accepted African American competitors, and it was one of the high points on the African American social calendar.

5. The Southeastern Pennsylvania Transportation Authority is of the largest transit systems in the United States, serving five counties in the Greater Philadelphia area and connecting to transit systems in Delaware and New Jersey. (septa.org/about)

6. Pronounced /jôn/ Dialect: chiefly in eastern Pennsylvania, jawn; noun: used to refer to a thing, place, person, or event that one need not or cannot give a specific name to.

7. Short for, The Atlanta University Center Consortium, which is the world's oldest and largest association of historically Black colleges and universities, comprising of four member institutions – Clark Atlanta University, Morehouse College, Morehouse School of Medicine, and Spelman College as of 2021.)

8. Maslow's hierarchy of needs is a charted set of human requirements that are important for an individual to achieve complete development and self-actualization. The hierarchy of needs is a theory of psychologist Abraham Maslow (https://whatis.techtarget.com/definition/Maslows-hierarchy-of-needs).

9. Papes: noun: Short for paper, as in paper money/bills.

10. Maat or Maʽat (Egyptian: mꜣꜥt /ˈmuʀʕat/, Coptic: ⲙⲉⲓ) refers to the ancient Egyptian concepts of truth, balance, order, harmony, law, morality, and justice.

Made in United States
Troutdale, OR
11/03/2026

56845402R00096